THE OPERATION OF AUTONOMOUS UNDERWATER VEHICLES

VOLUME THREE:
THE LAW GOVERNING AUV OPERATIONS - QUESTIONS AND ANSWERS

THE OPERATION OF AUTONOMOUS UNDERWATER VEHICLES

VOLUME THREE:
THE LAW GOVERNING AUV OPERATIONS - QUESTIONS AND ANSWERS

Prepared by

E D Brown

Professor of International Law in the University of Wales;
Director of the Centre for Marine Law & Policy, Cardiff University

and

N J J Gaskell

Professor of Maritime and Commercial Law
Institute of Maritime Law
University of Southampton

The Operation of Autonomous Underwater Vehicles Volume Three: The Law Governing AUV Operations – Questions and Answers
ISBN 0 906940 40 0

First published in 2001 by
The Society for Underwater Technology
80 Coleman Street, London EC2R 5BJ, UK

©2000 ED Brown & NJJ Gaskell

This publication is protected by international copyright law. All rights are reserved. No part of this publication may be reproduced or utilised in any form or by any means, electronic or mechanical including photocopying, recording or by any information storage and retrieval system, without the prior permission of the publishers.

Printed by Xerographic Printing Services Limited

Foreword

My purpose in commissioning this Question and Answer report from Professor Brown and Professor Gaskell was to provide the engineers and programme administrators working on the Natural Environment Research Council's Autosub projects with an easily accessible digest on the law relating to autonomous underwater vehicles. The questions have mostly come from the AUV community and reflect the concerns that they have about operating these novel vehicles in accordance with national and international law. Often, the answers reflect the immaturity of the technology and the fact that autonomous operation of vehicles has yet to make any significant impact on national or international law. Despite the resulting uncertainty, the authors have striven to give practical help to AUV users in this volume, while directing the reader requiring further details to their *Report on the Law* relating to the operation of autonomous underwater vehicles (Volume Two in this series).

Gwyn Griffiths
Southampton Oceanography Centre
June 2000

CONTENTS

Preface

Part A Introduction

1. What national maritime laws apply to AUVs?...11
2. What international maritime laws apply to AUVs?...11
3. How do AUVs relate to the draft Convention on Ocean Data Acquisition Systems (ODAS)?..13

Part B International Law of the Sea

4. What impact does UNCLOS have on the operation of AUVs?...........................15
5. What are the implications of the UNCLOS Maritime Zones for AUVs?............15
6. Will land locked neighbouring states need to be notified of AUV operations?....22
7. Whereas the rules of innocent passage require a submersible to transit on the surface, showing the flag, this would be difficult for an ocean science AUV. What other options could be considered?...23
8. Are there any special implications for AUV transits between zones?..................25
9. Does it matter legally what type of activity is undertaken by an AUV, e.g. whether it is performing marine scientific research (MSR) or commercial work?...26

Part C Operations in Particular Areas

10. What impact does the UK Antarctic Act (1994) have on AUV operations within the UK sector?..27
11. Do any special problems arise in relation to the deployment in Antarctica of AUVs launched from shore?..28
12. What other protocols, national, or international law may affect AUV operations in Antarctica?..30
13. Are there any special considerations for operations under ice shelves?.............31
14. What special problems might arise from operations within or close to shipping routes, either in 'open' waters or in straits (narrow straits such as Gibraltar and wider straits such as the Strait of Sicily)?...32

Part D Legal Definition of AUV

15. Under what circumstances and for which laws might an AUV be classed as a ship?..35
16. Is there any particular U.K. maritime legislation that could apply to AUVs?......43
17. What are the implications of an AUV being categorised as a 'ship' or not?........49
18. Is there a requirement in national or international law for an AUV to be registered?..50
19. What are the implications of registration or non-registration of an AUV?..........51
20. Is there a requirement in national or international law for an AUV to be classified, e.g. with Lloyd's Register, or is it advantageous to do so?...................53

Part E Legal Responsibilities

21. Do the master or owners of the vessel deploying an AUV have any legal responsibilities?...55
22. What sort of legal liabilities arise from the operation of AUVs?.........................55
23. What is the legal position of individuals working with AUVs (as opposed to that of their employers)? 56
24. Is there any difference between the legal position of an AUV owner, an AUV operator, an AUV hirer and an AUV manufacturer? 57
25. What are the liabilities of the Owners and Master of a vessel deploying an AUV? 58
26. What is the legal liability position where the owner of the AUV and the owner of the deploying vessel are same? 60
27. What is the legal liability position where the owner of the AUV hires in a deploying vessel?...60
28. What is the legal liability position where the owner of the AUV uses a deploying vessel belonging to a collaborating partner where no formal contract or agreement may exist?..61
29. Does the legal liability position vary where the owners of the AUV and the owner of the deploying vessel are in based in different States?......................................62
30. What are the liabilities of the manufacturer of the AUV? 63
31. What are the liabilities of a designer of an AUV where manufacture is entrusted or licensed to another?...64
32. What are the liabilities of the user of the AUV? 65
33. What are the liabilities of the person(s) programming the mission of the AUV?.66
34. Is there any special knowledge that the mission programmer should have in order to minimise legal liabilities? 67
35. How might these programming liabilities be affected if the AUV alters its own mission plan, e.g. due to a collision avoidance manoeuvre or due to feature tracking?...68
36. How might false claims for salvage be avoided?...68
37. Are there special contracts for using AUVs?...71
38. Do we always need a contract? 71
39. Do we have to employ a lawyer to draft AUV contracts? 72
40. When should we raise legal issues about contracts?..73
41. Which legal issues should we consider when drafting contracts involving AUVs? 73
42. Is it compulsory or merely advisable to insure an AUV? 74
43. How should AUV insurance be arranged and is there any special form of insurance for AUVs?..75

Part F Miscellaneous

44. What identification marks should an AUV carry and what warning signals should be provided when on the surface and when submerged?......................................77
45. If an AUV is launched from shore, how does this affect the issues discussed in this report?..79
46. How might legal disputes be settled?...80

Preface

In providing answers to questions put to them by AUV practitioners, it has been the objective of the authors of this publication to give concise, practical guidance on the law governing problems which may arise in the day-to-day management and operation of AUVs. The answers are relatively brief and, for the most part, include neither detailed citations of legal authority nor a full discussion of contentious points of law.

For a more extensive discussion of the questions considered in this publication and for guidance on numerous other legal issues arising from the operation of AUVs, the reader is referred to E D Brown and N J J Gaskell, *The Operation of Autonomous Underwater Vehicles, Volume Two: Report on the Law,* Society for Underwater Technology, 2000, referred to hereafter as *Report*. However, bearing in mind that the law in this area is complex and in certain respects uncertain, AUV operators should not rely on either the *Report* or the Answers provided here when addressing particular legal problems. Neither publication is intended as a substitute for full legal advice on particular issues arising in practice. In particular, national laws may vary considerably.

For the convenience of readers the Questions have been grouped under various sub-headings, which in part reflect the division of legal subject matter in the Report. It should be noted that that many of the questions raise issues which overlap legal categories, so that, for example, some issues of international law may arise in discussions about liability in national law, and vice versa.

E D Brown
N J J Gaskell
20 June 2000

Part A Introduction

1. What international maritime laws apply to AUVs?

Potentially, AUVs are governed by the general body of the rules of the international law of the sea to be found in both treaties and international customary law. The bulk of the rules are now embodied in the United Nations Convention on the Law of the Sea, 1982 (UNCLOS). Of particular interest to AUV operations are Part XIII of the Convention on Marine Scientific Research and Part XII on Protection and Preservation of the Marine Environment. However, many other Parts of UNCLOS are also relevant, including Parts II – VII, which deal with the delimitation and legal regimes of the various maritime zones from internal waters to the high seas.

The operation of AUVs is also governed by more specialised maritime law conventions (treaties), though the extent to which they apply to AUVs is in many cases uncertain and linked to the question whether or not AUVs are in law 'ships' (on which see *Report*, Section 6 and Question 9).

An attempt is made below in Question 15 to tabulate possibly relevant conventions such as the International Convention for the Safety of Life at Sea (SOLAS) and the Convention on the International Regulations for Preventing Collisions at Sea (COLREG), and to indicate the extent to which they may be applicable to AUVs. It has also to be noted that many international maritime laws may not apply to AUVs which are engaged in marine scientific research. See further *Report*, Sections 3.4 and 7.2 and Question 9.

AUVs may also be affected by regional agreements on the environment when operating in the regions covered by such instruments and by the various instruments of the Antarctic Treaty System.

See further *Report*, Part I, on 'The Public Law Regime Governing Autonomous Underwater Vehicles and Related State Practice and Procedure' and Part II, Sections 6 and 7, on international maritime conventions and their application to AUVs.

2. What national maritime laws apply to AUVs?

National variations. The operation of AUVs may potentially be subject to the national laws of any State in the world. Those laws could differ radically and may be subject to constant change. It may often only be possible to find out the applicable national law by making enquiries of local lawyers when a particular issue arises.

International harmonisation. A State might enact many different laws for its own territory but, owing to the international nature of shipping, it makes sense to achieve as much harmonisation as possible. For that reason States may agree international Conventions (treaties) between themselves. Examples include those agreed within the framework of the International Maritime Organisation, such as the International Convention on the Safety of Life at Sea 1974 (SOLAS). See further *Report* Section

7.3.1 and also Question 1, above. Most States give effect to Conventions by reproducing them in some way as part of their national law.

Form of national law. A U.K. operator would primarily look to a U.K. enactment, although it will often be based on an international Convention also applied by other States. Most modern U.K. Acts (such as the Merchant Shipping Act 1995) give the Government the power to issue Regulations which will contain the continually changing detailed rules, e.g. on matters of construction, derived from the international Conventions. There may also be local legislation applying in ports, e.g. bylaws, which may give extensive powers to harbour masters. In so-called "common law" States (including the U.K.) the legislation is supplemented by principles laid down by judges in case law.

Whose law? National laws of a particular State will usually be applied to an AUV, and those operating it, when it is "within the jurisdiction" of that State. Normally this means when it is within the territorial limit of that State (usually 12 miles, but see Question 1, above). The national laws of a State may apply sometimes even when there is no physical presence in that State. States claim the right to regulate the activities of their nationals (including companies) and craft operating anywhere in the world. In the case of ships, this is referred to as "flag state control": i.e. control is exercised by the State of the ship's flag (usually where it is registered). It is to be contrasted with "port state control", which is where States apply their national rules when foreign ships visit their ports. In contracts concerning AUVs, the parties may have chosen that the law of one State (commonly English law in maritime contracts) should be used to solve any disputes, wherever any incident occurs. See *Report* Section 11.4.6. Where there is a casualty causing loss or injury, it will usually be the national law of the place of that loss or injury which applies. Some States apply their national law very widely, even in circumstances where there is only a small connection between an incident and that State. In practice, it is important to note that where claimants can persuade US courts to assume jurisdiction over such a case this can have important consequences in terms of the amount of damages awarded and this factor may well affect insurance costs: see further, Question 17, below.

Types of national law. There are different types of national law which could apply to AUVs. Many of these could apply equally to the operation of land based vehicles, e.g. employment laws. Our search is for any laws which apply specifically to AUVs themselves, or for those general maritime laws (designed for ships) which can by analogy be applied to AUVs because they should be treated as 'ships'. As AUVs are a novel category of craft, there are few, if any, laws specifically designed for them. For that reason, it is necessary to see how far they can be treated as 'ships' in maritime law. There is no simple universal answer that can be given to that question, although it appears that most will not be treated as ships: see further, Questions 15-17, below.
For convenience, the types of law applicable to AUVs can be placed in very broad categories:

> *Regulatory laws*: There are public regulatory rules applying to those who operate ships. These may lay down construction or operational standards and will be enforced by the criminal law. There may often be detailed powers of control given to ports or local public authorities. A State may also reserve to itself large powers to intervene in casualties which might threaten life or

	the environment. It is entirely possible that many AUVs are not yet caught by the detailed rules designed for ships. It is necessary to look at each separate enactment to be sure if it applies. See further *Report* Sections 7.1, 7.3.24.
Contract laws:	In general, there is nothing special about AUV contracts and, when contracts are made by AUV operators, normal national contract laws apply. They may even apply to quite informal agreements between scientific institutions for the use of equipment. In practice, most operators will rely on standard form, pre-drafted contracts: see further *Report* Section 11.
Liability laws:	If AUVs cause property damage or injury to third parties, a variety of national liability laws could apply. Although recent legislation (e.g. to protect the environment) may create "strict" liability, most liability laws will probably require proof of fault. See further *Report* Section 10.
Maritime laws:	Every international maritime Convention in a sense creates new maritime law, but there are some laws which create obligations or grant rights which are different from those for land operations. Salvage law is an example. See further *Report* Sections 10.2.3, 12.2, 9.4.

U.K. regulatory law. The question of whether general U.K. maritime regulatory law will apply to AUVs depends on whether they are classified as "ships" within s. 313(1) of the Merchant Shipping Act 1995. It is not possible to be definite without a court ruling, but it appears that English law will *not* generally apply to AUVs (which are incapable of carrying humans) those laws and regulations which apply to 'ships'. See further *Report* Section 6.4. Under s. 311 of the Merchant Shipping Act 1995 the U.K. could issue an Order declaring that an AUV is to be treated as a 'ship', but there are no plans to do so at present. Such action is likely to be taken only if there is an AUV incident raising safety or environmental issues. See further *Report* Section 6.5.

The consequence of not treating AUVs as ships for regulatory purposes is that many detailed construction and operational requirements (e.g. those for manned submersibles) do not apply to AUVs at present. But it is necessary to look at each Convention and each national regulation to see if some more specific rule has been made applying to AUVs. See further *Report* Sections 7.1, 7.3.24. Thus, even though not ships, AUVs are subject to the law of salvage (*Report* Sections 10.2.3, 7.3.18).
Other national regulatory laws. Other legal systems may have different national laws which *do* apply specific regulations to AUVs.

Marine scientific research. Note that many maritime laws may not apply to AUVs engaged in MSR: see further *Report* Sections 3.4, 7.2 and Question 9.

3. How do AUVs relate to the draft Convention on Ocean Data Acquisition Systems (ODAS)?

Pending the completion and entry into force of a Convention on Ocean Data Acquisition Systems (ODAS), which is not imminent, the draft Convention has no impact upon the operation of AUVs. A review of the relevant proceedings of the

International Oceanographic Commission (IOC) and the International Maritime Organisation (IMO) on this question suggests that, although the Russian Delegation to IOC is still pressing to proceed with further work on a draft Convention, there appears to be a marked disinclination among other Governments to take the matter further. In any event, it is clear that a great deal of work would need to be done on the draft provisions, including in particular those dealing with liability. Pending the concentration of minds which might result from a serious incident involving an AUV, the prevailing view seems to favour letting sleeping dogs lie.

However, mention has also to be made of the three Technical Annexes to the draft Convention which were published on behalf of UNESCO and IMO in 1972 so that, pending the conclusion of the Convention, States could use them, on a voluntary basis, as guidelines for national measures. The Annexes deal with *Notification* (Annex I), *Marking and Signals* (Annex II), and *Construction Arrangements and Other Safety Provisions* (Annex III). An updated version of Annex II was circulated to IMO Member States in 1985.

For detailed discussion, see further:

- *Report,* Section 3.3: *Drafting a convention on the legal status of ODAS.* Appendices IA and IB to the *Report* contain the texts of the original three Technical Annexes and the revised version of Technical Annex II.
- *Report*, Section 8, on the provisions of the draft ODAS Convention dealing with liabilities.
- Question 44: What identification marks should an AUV carry and what warning signals should be provided when on the surface and when submerged?; and
- Question 7, so far as it refers to the rule requiring a ship in innocent passage to show its flag.

Part B International Law of the Sea

4. What impact does UNCLOS have on the operation of AUVs?

The United Nations Convention on the Law of the Sea, 1982 (UNCLOS) lays down the framework of rules of international law which States have to observe when operating or regulating the operation of AUVs. The various Parts of UNCLOS deal with such matters as national maritime zones (delimitation and use of), conduct of marine scientific research (MSR), the freedoms of the high seas (including the freedoms of navigation and of MSR), protection of the environment, nationality of ships and safety at sea.

The impact of UNCLOS on the operation of AUVs will most often be indirect. The rules of international law, of which UNCLOS is part, are binding upon States and will typically be applied to operators of AUVs through national legislation or codes of practice. For example, questions relating to the status of AUVs (is it a ship, vessel, submersible or whatever?) and their safety will be dealt with in Merchant Shipping legislation, based upon UNCLOS and, very often, other supplementary and more specialised treaties. Questions relating to access to foreign waters to conduct MSR may also be dealt with in national legislation implementing UNCLOS rules on MSR and jurisdiction in maritime zones; or they may be covered by administrative procedures or codes of practice of a less formal kind.

For detailed discussion, see further:

- On *Maritime Zones*, *Report*, Section 1.
- On *Jurisdiction over MSR in maritime zones*, *Report*, Section 3.2.2.
- On *Scientific research installations or equipment in the marine environment*, *Report*, Section 3.2.4, and Question 3 above.

5. What are the implications of the UNCLOS Maritime Zones for AUVs?

Under the United Nations Convention on the Law of the Sea, 1982 (UNCLOS), the seas are divided horizontally into nine jurisdictional zones. In some case different jurisdictional regimes apply in the three vertical subdivisions of these zones. These zones are as shown in Table 1.

The coastal State has jurisdiction (the extent of which varies from zone to zone) over Zones 1 – 7. In Zone 8, the high seas, all States enjoy the freedom of the high seas but in Zone 9 (the Area of the seabed beyond the outer limit of the continental shelf) a special regime applies to seabed mining, administered by the International Seabed Authority.

UNCLOS has established a regime governing the conduct of MSR in the various maritime zones, whether carried out by research vessels or AUVs. As will be seen, the degree of control that the coastal State may exercise over MSR diminishes as we move from land to high seas. Thus, at one extreme, the coastal State has full sovereignty over MSR conducted by foreign vessels in its internal waters but, at the other extreme, has no jurisdiction over MSR conducted by foreign vessels on the high seas. In the middle, in the exclusive economic zone (EEZ) and on the continental shelf, a 'qualified consent' regime applies and the coastal State has only limited jurisdiction over such research.

The implications for AUVs may be summarised as follows:

Internal waters (Zones 1A, 1B and 1C)

The coastal State has full sovereignty over internal waters, that is, all waters landward of the baselines of the territorial sea. It follows that no MSR may be conducted by AUVs in the internal waters of a foreign State without its consent.

Archipelagic waters (Zones 2A, 2B and 2C)

Under Part IV of UNCLOS an 'archipelagic State' (a State such as Indonesia which is constituted wholly or mainly by one or more archipelagos) may draw 'archipelagic straight baselines' around its archipelago/s and the enclosed waters have the status of 'archipelagic waters'. The archipelagic State has sovereignty over its archipelagic waters and foreign ships or AUVs may not carry out research in these waters without the prior authorisation of the archipelagic State.

Territorial sea (Zones 3A, 3B and 3C)

The coastal State has sovereignty over the territorial sea extending to a maximum breadth of 12 nm. Accordingly, Article 245 of UNCLOS provides that:

> Coastal States, in the exercise of their sovereignty, have the exclusive right to regulate, authorise and conduct marine scientific research in their territorial sea. Marine scientific research therein shall be conducted only with the express consent of and under the conditions set forth by the coastal State.

Thus, AUVs may conduct MSR in the territorial sea of a foreign State only with its express consent.

Contiguous zone (Zone 4A, 4B and 4C)

Under Article 33 of UNCLOS, the coastal State may exercise certain controls in a contiguous zone adjacent to the territorial sea and extending to a maximum breadth of 24 miles from territorial sea baselines. However, these controls do not relate to MSR and, for purposes of jurisdiction over MSR, the waters of the contiguous zone retain the status of an EEZ (if the coastal Sate has claimed an EEZ) or of the high seas (if not).

TABLE 1: MARITIME ZONES

	Internal Waters	Archipelagic Waters	Territorial Sea	Contiguous Zone	Exclusive Fishing Zone	Exclusive Economic Zone	Continental Shelf	High Seas	The Area
Water Column	1A	2A	3A	4A	5A	6A	7A	8A	9A
Seabed	1B	2B	3B	4B	5B	6B	7B	8B	9B
Subsoil	1C	2C	3C	4C	5C	6C	7C	8C	9C

Exclusive fishing zone (Zones 5A, 5B and 5C)

The concept of the exclusive fishing zone is not recognised in UNCLOS but its existence has been acknowledge by the International Court of Justice and, of course, many States, including the United Kingdom, claim an exclusive fishing zone and do not claim the more comprehensive exclusive economic zone. While the coastal State may doubtless claim jurisdiction over research related to the exploitation of fish in the exclusive fishing zone, such research is beyond the scope of this paper. Since the area of the exclusive fishing zone will normally overlap the area of the legal continental shelf, the coastal State may have certain jurisdictional powers over MSR in the waters of this zone. However, these powers are properly considered below under the heading of the continental shelf.

Exclusive economic zone (Zones 6A, 6B and 6C) and continental shelf (Zones 7A, 7B and 7C)

Given the fact that UNCLOS deals with MSR in the EEZ and on the continental shelf together in Article 246, it is convenient to consider them together here too.

The detailed rules governing MSR in the EEZ and on the continental shelf are in Part XIII of the UN Convention – 'Marine Scientific Research'. They may be summarised as follows:

- *The general principle – a qualified consent regime*

While it is true that the coastal State has the right to regulate and authorise MSR in its EEZ or on its continental shelf and that such MSR may be conducted only with its consent, it does not have an absolute discretion to withhold consent. The general rule is that in 'normal circumstances' consent has to be granted for MSR carried out 'for peaceful purposes and in order to increase scientific knowledge of the marine environment for the benefit of all mankind'. The coastal State is given a discretion to withhold consent in specified circumstances and to suspend or terminate MSR in other cases. Nonetheless, the underlying policy reflected in these provisions is in favour of consent being granted and, indeed, the coastal State is required to establish rules and procedures to ensure that consent will not be delayed or denied unreasonably. Although 'normal circumstances' are not defined, they may exist in spite of the absence of diplomatic relations between the coastal and researching States.

- *How to apply for consent*

Applications have to be submitted through 'appropriate official channels', unless otherwise agreed by the States concerned. The application has to be received by the coastal State not less than six months before the expected start of the MSR project and has to contain a full description of:

(a) the nature and objectives of the project;

(b) the method and means to be used, including name, tonnage, type and class of vessels and a description of scientific equipment;

(c) the precise geographical areas in which the project is to be conducted;

(d) The expected date of first appearance and final departure of the research vessels, or deployment of the equipment and its removal, as appropriate;

(e) the name of the sponsoring institution, its director, and the person in charge of the project; and

(f) the extent to which it is considered that the coastal State should be able to participate or to be represented in the project.

- *Conditions to be complied with in conducting MSR*

Under Article 249(1), the researching State has to comply with the following conditions:

(a) ensure the right of the coastal State, if it so desires, to participate or be represented in the marine scientific research project, especially on board research vessels and other craft or scientific research installations, when practicable, without payment of any remuneration to the scientists of the coastal State and without obligation to contribute towards the costs of the project;

(b) provide the coastal State, at its request, with preliminary reports, as soon as practicable, and with the final results and conclusions after the completion of the research;

(c) undertake to provide access for the coastal State, at its request, to all data and samples derived from the marine scientific research project and likewise to furnish it with data which may be copied and samples which may be divided without detriment to their scientific value;

(d) if requested, provide the coastal Sate with an assessment of such data, samples and research results or provide assistance in their assessment or interpretation;

(e) ensure that the research results are made internationally available through appropriate national or international channels, as soon as practicable;

(f) inform the coastal State immediately of any major change in the research programme;

(g) unless otherwise agreed, remove the scientific research installations or equipment once the research is completed.

It is open to the coastal State to withhold consent if the project is of direct significance for the exploration and exploitation of natural resources, living or non-living. If, nonetheless, consent is granted it may be subject to the condition that the results of the research may be made internationally available only with the prior agreement of the coastal State.

Finally, MSR activities must not unjustifiably interfere with activities undertaken by the coastal State in the exercise of its sovereign rights and jurisdiction in the EEZ and on the continental shelf.

It should be emphasised that the researching State has a clear international legal duty to ensure compliance with these various conditions. Failure to do so may seriously prejudice freedom of MSR in foreign waters. There are many loopholes which can be used by the coastal State to frustrate the effective operation of this consent regime and it is essential that a climate of trust is established by ensuring that principal scientists and civil servants comply fully and in good faith with these conditions. Understandably, scientists frequently find compliance with such conditions irksome, especially in the context of relations with an inefficient or unhelpful foreign bureaucracy. Nonetheless, it should be remembered that the cost of failure to comply may well be an inability to secure consent for a later project.

- *Implied consent*

Reflecting the Convention's positive attitude to MSR and recognising that it should not be frustrated by the failure of the coastal State to respond in a timely fashion, provision is made for implied consent in Article 252.

- *Discretion to withhold consent*

Consent may be withheld in the various circumstances specified in Article 246(5) of UNCLOS.

- *Suspension or cessation of MSR project*

Suspension or cessation of an MSR project may be required by the coastal State in the situations specified in Article 253.

- *MSR in continental shelf beyond 200 nm line*

In areas where the continental margin extends beyond the 200 nm outer limit of the EEZ, the coastal State is entitled to extend its legal continental shelf to the outer edge of the continental margin. However, the water column above that part of the continental shelf which lies seaward of this 200 nm limit retains the legal status of high seas and it is accordingly provided in Article 257 that all States have the right to conduct MSR in this water column. Needless to say, this rule applies only to Zone 7A.

As regards Zones 7B and 7C, that is, the seabed and subsoil of this area of the continental shelf, the Convention offers a useful concession in favour of freedom of MSR. One of the grounds on which the coastal State may normally withhold consent is that the project is of direct significance for the exploration and exploitation of natural resources of the continental shelf. Where, however, the project is to be undertaken on that part of the continental shelf which lies beyond the 200 nm line, the coastal State may not withhold its consent on that ground unless the research is to be conducted within specific areas designated by the coastal State as areas in which exploitation or detailed exploratory operations are occurring or will occur within a reasonable period of time. This rule is of course without prejudice to the rights of coastal States over the continental shelf.

- *Measures to facilitate MSR and port calls*

Port calls are often a useful facility and sometimes a necessary part of an MSR expedition. It is, therefore, useful to have the following 'measures to facilitate marine scientific research and assist research vessels' prescribed in Article 255:

> States shall endeavour to adopt reasonable rules, regulations and procedures to promote and facilitate marine scientific research conducted in accordance with this Convention beyond their territorial sea and, as appropriate, to facilitate, subject to the provisions of their laws and regulations, access to their harbours and promote assistance for marine scientific research vessels which comply with the relevant provisions of this Part.

These provisions do of course apply principally to research vessels but may indirectly benefit AUVs associated with them.

The high seas (Zone 8A)

Freedom of scientific research is expressly included among the six freedoms of the high seas listed in Article 87(1) of UNCLOS and would be enjoyed by AUVs. Such freedom has to be exercised with 'due regard' for the interests of other States in their exercise of the freedom of the high seas. It is added that due regard must be had too 'to the rights under this Convention with respect to activities in the Area'.

The 'Area' beyond the limits of national jurisdiction (Zone 9B and 9C)

The 'Area' referred to is the area of the seabed and ocean floor and subsoil thereof lying seaward of the outer limit of the legal continental shelf. It is the area to which the seabed mining regime contained in Part XI of UNCLOS applies. Provision is made in UNCLOS for MSR to be conducted by the International Seabed Authority and by States. Although the scope of these provisions is in doubt, it would appear that there should be no serious impediment to MSR carried out by AUVs operated by entities other than the Authority in the Area and in the superjacent water column if it is conducted in compliance with Article 147. Under paragraph 1 of that article, seabed mining activities in the Area must be carried out with reasonable regard for other activities in the marine environment (which would include MSR by AUVs). Correspondingly, paragraph 3 demands that other activities (which would include MSR by AUVs) in the marine environment must be conducted with reasonable regard for seabed mining activities in the Area.

For detailed discussion, see further:

- On *Maritime Zones*, Report, Section 1. The best source of information on national claims to maritime zones is the *Law of the Sea Bulletin* (Division for Ocean Affairs and the Law of the Sea, Office of Legal Affairs, United Nations) which regularly publishes a table of claims to maritime zones, as well as reporting in every issue on more recent claims. The most recent 'Table of claims to maritime zones' is in *Bulletin* No. 39 (1999), pp. 40-50.

- On *Jurisdiction over MSR in maritime zones, Report*, Section 3.2.2.
- On *Scientific research installations or equipment in the marine environment, Report*, Section 3.2.4.

6. Will land-locked neighbouring States need to be notified of AUV operations?

UNCLOS grants a privileged position both to land-locked States (L-L States) and geographically disadvantaged States (G-D States). The L-L State is defined simply as 'a State which has no sea-coast'. G-D States are defined, in relation to their rights in the EEZ, as 'coastal States, including States bordering enclosed or semi-enclosed seas, whose geographical situation makes them dependent upon the exploitation of the living resources of the exclusive economic zones of other States in the subregion or region for adequate supplies of fish for the nutritional purposes of their populations or part thereof, and coastal States which can claim no exclusive zones of their own'.

Such States enjoy certain rights to participate in MSR projects under Article 254 of UNCLOS and to benefit from technical co-operation and assistance in relation to MSR under Article 266, as indicated below:

- *Right to receive notice of proposed MSR projects*

States and international organisations submitting proposals to coastal States to undertake MSR projects in their EEZs or on their continental shelf exclusively for peaceful purposes and in order to increase scientific knowledge of the marine environment for the benefit of mankind, are required to give notice to the neighbouring L-L and G-D States of the proposed research project. No time is specified for giving such notice other than is suggested by the fact that the 'States …which *have submitted…* a project … *shall give* notice …'

- *Right to receive information on project*

Once consent has been granted to the researching State, it must provide to neighbouring L-L and G-D States, *at their request and when appropriate*, the same information as it is required to provide to the coastal State. The information, which must be provided not less than 6 months in advance of the expected starting date of the MSR project, consists of a full description of the project, including the methods and means to be used and a description of scientific equipment. Any major change in the research programme has also to be notified.

- *Right to participate in project*

L-L and G-D States have to be given the opportunity to participate in the project but the right is a highly qualified one. The opportunity will be given at their request, but only 'whenever feasible'. The opportunity is to be enjoyed 'through qualified experts appointed by them and not objected to by the coastal State'. Finally, the opportunity to participate must be 'in accordance with the conditions agreed for the project, in conformity with the provisions of UNCLOS, between the coastal State and the researching State.

- *Right to assistance in interpreting research*

The researching State must provide L-L and G-D States at their request with an assessment of the project's data, samples and research results or provide assistance in their assessment or interpretation. However, this obligation is qualified by reference to the provisions of Article 249(2), which enables the coastal State in certain circumstances to require its prior agreement for making internationally available the research results of a project of direct significance for the exploration and exploitation of natural resources.

- *Qualified nature of rights of L-L and G-D States*

Summing up, although it is true that these States are the beneficiaries of a number of rights in relation to (i) notice of, (ii) information on, and (iii) participation in MSR projects in the waters of neighbouring States, and are further entitled to (iv) assistance in interpreting the results of such research, these rights are subject to a number of conditions which may allow the researching State to avoid the assumption of heavy burdens in certain circumstances. This is particularly so in relation to the right to participate in projects.

For more detailed discussion, see further *Report*, Section 3.2.3.

7. Whereas the rules on innocent passage require a submersible to navigate on the surface, showing the flag, this would be difficult for an ocean science AUV. What other options could be considered?

The rules on innocent passage are now codified in the United Nations Convention on the Law of the Sea, 1982 (UNCLOS), which lays down rules for innocent passage through (i) the territorial sea; (ii) straits used for international navigation; and (iii) archipelagic waters.

The basic rule referred to in the question is to be found in Article 20 of UNCLOS, which deals with the innocent passage of *Submarines and other underwater vehicles* in the territorial sea and requires that they 'navigate on the surface and show their flag'. The later articles dealing with innocent passage through straits (Article 45) and through archipelagic waters (Article 52) incorporate the same requirements by making a cross-reference to this basic rule.

In addressing this question, it has first to be noted that the basic rule in Article 20 is part of a subsection of UNCLOS containing 'Rules applicable to all *ships*' (emphasis added) and it follows that an AUV will only enjoy the right of innocent passage if it may properly be classified in law as a ship. It is my no means clear that this is so.

Assuming that the AUV does have a right of innocent passage, and that navigation on the surface and showing the flag are difficult, what other options may be open to the AUV operator?

If all that is required is a right to traverse the territorial sea without undertaking any ocean science research, it might be possible to secure the coastal State's consent to submerged passage by negotiations. It seems likely that the coastal State would attach conditions to any such consent, including, possibly, indemnification against any claim in respect of damage caused to third parties by the AUV. The coastal State might also adapt the model offered by Article 16 of the draft Convention on ODAS. It requires that a submarine ODAS which, due to the depth at which it is deployed, 'constitutes a danger to shipping or navigation or to fishing', must either be escorted by a vessel capable of giving due warning to passing ships, or be provided with effective signals as set forth in Annex II.

Another alternative, of course (bearing in mind that passage and not research is the object of the exercise), would be for the AUV to be carried through the waters in question as cargo or equipment of a merchant vessel or a research vessel.

As regards the requirement that the AUV should show its flag, this is a clear, unambiguous requirement of UNCLOS and not an alternative to the 'effective signals' envisaged by the draft Convention on ODAS. Its purpose is to identify the national character of the vessel, whereas signals are, of course, designed for safety purposes. Needless to say, the flag requirement would apply only to that part of any passage undertaken on the surface.

It may not be beyond the wit of man to devise some sort of 'pop-up' flag for AUVs. However, not only would this be a wasteful use of scarce space and an added design complication, but it would probably also be impracticable to devise a flag of such dimensions as to be usefully visible. Fortunately, there is an alternative which, though not perhaps strictly meeting the UNCLOS requirement, would probably not cause difficulties in practice.

Reference was made above, in the Answer to Question 3, to the Technical Annexes to the draft Convention on ODAS which were published separately so that, pending the conclusion of a Convention, States could use them on a voluntary basis as guidelines for national measures. As was seen, an updated version of Annex II on *Marking and Signals* was circulated in 1985 and one of the changes which it introduced may well provide a solution to the flag problem. Paragraph 1.1.1 first makes provision for the display on the exterior of the ODAS of 'a unique identification number prefixed by the letters ODAS and suffixed by letters indicating the State in which' it is registered. It is then added in Paragraph 1.1.3, however, that, 'A replica of the flag of the State in which the ODAS is registered may also be painted on or applied to the exterior surface as a further optional means of identification'. In requesting the coastal State to consent to the submarine passage of an AUV, it would be prudent to seek its confirmation of the acceptability of this method of 'showing its flag' in relation to any part of the passage made on the surface.

For detailed discussion, see further:

- On *Jurisdiction over Marine Scientific Research in maritime zones*, *Report*, Section 3.2.2.
- On the question of *What is a Ship?*, *Report*, Section 6.
- On the *draft Convention on ODAS and its Technical Annexes*, *Report*, Section 3.3 and Question 3 above.

8. Are there any special implications for AUV passage between zones?

There are possibly two questions here. First, if, in carrying out research, an AUV would, or possibly might, operate in more than one maritime zone, are there any special implications? Secondly, if, in travelling to or returning from research activities, an AUV passes though more than one maritime zone, are there any special implications?

If the AUV is to conduct research activities in more than one maritime zone, the only implication is that it will be necessary to ensure that the rules governing MSR in the various maritime zones are complied with. For example, if a British AUV is to conduct research in the adjacent territorial seas and EEZs of States A and B, the consent of the authorities in States A and B must be secured in accordance with the rules outlined in the Answer to Question 5 above. Common sense would also dictate that if, intentionally or accidentally, there is any chance that the AUV's data gathering will extend into other zones, the request(s) for consent should extend geographically to cover these zones too.

So far as passage to and from research sites is concerned, much will depend not only on what zones are involved but also on the question whether an AUV is a ship and the attitude of any coastal State involved to that question.

If the AUV is considered to be a ship and this proposition is accepted by relevant coastal States, the AUV would enjoy rights of innocent passage (see Question 7) through the territorial sea; 'transit passage' (which is more extensive than innocent passage and includes submerged passage) through most territorial sea straits; innocent passage and 'archipelagic sealanes passage' (surface or submerged) through archipelagic waters; and freedom of navigation (surface or submerged) in zones seaward of the outer limit of the territorial sea.

If, on the other hand, the view is taken that an AUV is not a ship, the legal position is much less clear. The various rights of passage referred to above are enjoyed by ships, which are of course subject to national and international shipping law on such matters as safety, protection of the environment, collisions and liability. Pending the development of clearer rules governing AUVs, it would be prudent for AUVs to be transported to and from research areas by mother ships.

For more detailed discussion, see further:

- On securing consent for MSR in the various maritime zones, *Report*, Section 3.2.2 and Question 5 above.

9 Does it matter legally what type of activity is undertaken by an AUV, for example, whether it is performing MSR or commercial work?

The type of activity undertaken by an AUV may be legally relevant in the context of possible claims to sovereign immunity for AUV MSR activities. It may also be relevant to the application of particular maritime conventions.

Both the general rules of the international law of the sea and a number of international shipping law conventions recognise that ships owned or operated by a State and used only on government non-commercial service enjoy sovereign immunity from the jurisdiction of other States. In most cases this does not mean that such ships are immune from the obligation to comply with the substantive rules of law in question; the immunity is rather from the exercise of any form of jurisdiction or legal process over them by a foreign State. Nonetheless, it is important to be aware of the scope and meaning of such immunity, particularly in relation to the question whether AUVs are in law to be classified as ships and thus subject to the provisions of shipping law conventions.

In considering the possible relevance of the rules on sovereign immunity for the legal regime governing the operation of AUVs for the purpose of marine scientific research, two main questions are likely to arise in concrete cases. First, is the AUV owned or operated by the State?; and secondly, is the AUV employed on non-commercial service? In theory, both questions can raise difficult issues (see further *Report*, Section 3.4, 7.2). However, in practice, there will frequently be at least two good reasons for not claiming immune status. First and foremost, foreign States may be less sympathetic to requests for consent to undertake MSR in their waters if the request is made by an agency for which sovereign immunity is claimed. Secondly, in the real world of MSR, it is not always easy to classify particular missions as being entirely non-commercial and, in such cases, claims to sovereign immunity would be difficult to sustain. It may well be that it is considerations such as those which have determined policy in the United Kingdom on the status of NERC. It is understood that immunity is not claimed for this Non-Departmental Public Body.

Even if sovereign immunity is not claimed, it may be that a particular maritime statute or convention is expressed not to apply to MSR activities in any event.

For application of specific conventions to MSR, see Question 15, col. 3

Part C Operations in Particular Areas

10. What impact does the UK Antarctic Act (1994) have on AUV operations within the UK sector?

The Antarctic Act 1994 and the Antarctic Regulations 1995 made under it apply to Antarctica, as defined in the Act, which includes the British sector. It follows that any person on a British expedition to Antarctica and any British vessel entering the British sector would be subject to the national law regime established by these instruments. The principal elements of the regime which may impact upon AUV operations may be summarised as follows:

- *The permits system*
  Provision is made in several sections of the Act requiring permits to be obtained for various activities in Antarctica. The number and type of permits required depend upon the nature of the activity in question.
- *Conservation of Antarctic fauna and flora*
  In the interests of the conservation of Antarctic fauna and flora, UK nationals are forbidden to do various things in Antarctica except under a permit granted under the Act or under a written authorisation from another State Party to the 1991 Protocol on Environmental Protection to the Antarctic Treaty. The forbidden activities include 'use of a vehicle, vessel or aircraft in a manner that disturbs a concentration of native mammals or native birds' and doing 'anything that is likely to cause significant damage to the habitat of any native mammal, bird, plant or invertebrate'.
- *Special areas*
  The Act makes provision for two types of special area, areas restricted under the 1991 Protocol and places protected under a 1980 Convention for the Conservation of Antarctic Marine Living Resources (CCAMLR). Permits are required for entry into such special areas.
- *Environmental evaluations*
  In applying an Environmental Impact Assessment procedure introduced by the 1991 Protocol, the UK's 1995 Antarctic Regulations distinguish between:
  (i) activities likely to have a negligible impact on the environment, for which neither an Initial Environmental Evaluation (IEE) nor a Comprehensive Environmental Evaluation (CEE) is required;
  (ii) 'activities likely to have more than a negligible impact', referred to in the Protocol as a 'minor or transitory impact'. For such activities an IEE will normally have to be submitted, though the Secretary of State can require a draft CEE; and
  (iii) 'activities likely to have more than a minor or transitory impact'. For this level of expected impact, a draft CEE must be submitted, followed later by a final CEE which has to take account of comments and advice from various sources.

Whether the AUV in question were to be classified as a 'vehicle' or a 'vessel', it would be subject to the above regime (including whatever permits conditions as might be imposed) if operated in Antarctica by any person on a British expedition or from a British vessel.

For more detailed discussion, see:

- On the regime governing marine science research and the deployment of AUVs in Antarctica, *Report*, Section 5.
- On the Antarctic Act 1994 and the Antarctic Regulations 1995, *Report*, sections 5.5.1 and 5.5.2.
- On the position of AUVs launched from shore in Antarctica, Question 11 below.
- Appendix III to the *Report* which contains official U.K. Permit Application Forms and Guidance Notes for Expeditions to Antarctica.

11. Do any special problems arise in relation to the deployment in Antarctica of AUVs launched from shore?

The legal status of AUVs under United Kingdom law is unclear and, consequently, the law and procedure relating to AUVs launched from shore in Antarctica is uncertain. It would seem advisable to consider two possibilities: (1) that an AUV is, or might in future be treated as, a ship in law; and (2) that an AUV is not a ship in law.

1. Assuming the AUV is or might in future be treated as a ship in law

If an AUV may properly be regarded as being a 'ship' in law, its entry into, and deployment from shore in, Antarctica would be subject to the same rules as apply to more conventional Marine Scientific Research (MSR) ships operating in this area, including section 5(1) of the Antarctic Act 1994, under which a 'British vessel' may not enter Antarctica without a permit. It is difficult to accept that, at the present time, an AUV is in law a ship as generally understood in British maritime law and it will therefore be necessary to consider below the consequences which would flow from a finding that an AUV is not in law a ship. Before doing so, however, it should be noted that, even if it is accepted that an AUV is not a ship in law under current law, it might in future be treated as a ship if the Secretary of State exercises his powers under section 311(1) of the Merchant Shipping Act 1995 (MSA 95). The argument is as follows. Under section 5(3) of the Antarctic Act 1994, a 'British vessel' means a 'United Kingdom ship' within the meaning of section 85(2) of MSA 95.[*] Under this subsection, a 'United Kingdom ship' is a ship which -

(a) is registered in the United Kingdom; or
(b) is not registered under the law of any country but is wholly owned by persons each of whom is –
   (i) a British citizen, a British Dependent Territories citizen or a British Overseas citizen, or
   (ii) a body corporate which is established under the law of a part of the United Kingdom and has its principal place of business in the United Kingdom.

---

[*] The original reference in s.5(3) of the Antarctic Act was to s.21(1) of MSA 79, repealed by MSA 95, s.314 and Sch. 12.

It is open to the Secretary of State under section 311(1) of MSA 95 to make an order providing that an AUV (being 'a thing designed or adapted for use at sea') is to be treated as a ship for the purposes of section 85(2). Moreover, since, under section 311(2)(a), the order may 'make different provision in relation to different occasions', it would probably be possible for the order to specify that the designation of the AUV as a ship was for the purposes of the interpretation and application of section 5 of the Antarctic Act 1994. In these circumstances, the AUV would be treated like any other MSR ship in Antarctica and its launch from shore would raise no special problems. The operator would, of course, have to apply for a permit which would be granted only after consideration of an environmental impact assessment (EIA). As it is put in the *Guide to Environmental Impact Assessment of Activities in Antarctica* (FCO, 1995, at p.3), '…the carrying out of an EIA will be a precondition for the grant of a permit'.

2. Assuming the AUV is not a ship in law

Assuming that the AUV is not a ship under current law and that no order to treat it as a ship has been made under section 311(1) of MSA 95, the legal position is much less clear. What is clear, however, is that a permit would be required for the MSR mission of the AUV in Antarctica, including its launch from shore. Since the AUV is assumed not to be a ship, it cannot be a 'British vessel' under section 5(1) of the Antarctic Act 1994 and, therefore, there can be no question of applying for a permit under that section. It would appear therefore that a permit would have to be applied for under section 3 of the Antarctic Act 1994 which applies to all 'British expeditions to Antarctica'.

The standard application form for section 3 applications is reproduced, together with Guidance Notes, in *Report*, Appendix III(1). Paragraph 2 requires information to be given on the 'purpose of the expedition' and Paragraph 23 seeks information on any EIA conducted for the expedition. How would an AUV fit into this framework? One possibility is that it would simply be treated as a research tool or instrument and that its potential impact on the environment would be evaluated in an EIA as one, albeit a very important, element of the proposed research activities. If more than a 'negligible impact on the environment' was anticipated, it would be open to the Secretary of State to require either an Initial Environmental Evaluation or the more demanding Comprehensive Environmental Evaluation (see further *Report*, Section 5.5.2.2). Moreover, it is also open to the Minister, under section 13(1), to attach to any permit whatever conditions are thought fit, thus making possible the provision of a further set of safeguards.

Given the fact that the spirit of the Antarctic regime is pro-Marine Scientific Research, it seems reasonable to expect that the approach outlined above would be adopted by the Secretary of State. There is, however, another possibility. As has been seen, it is a fine question whether the AUV is a 'ship' or not and it might therefore be thought to be contrary to the spirit of the Antarctic Act if AUVs were not subject to the same controls as ships. Given the autonomous characteristics of AUVs, their relative lack of an environmental track record, and the fact that a mother ship would offer safeguards otherwise absent, it is possible that a permit would be refused in cases where the AUV was shore-launched and not supervised from an attendant mother ship. It may be noted in this context that the *FCO Guide* (p.6, para. 11.1), in outlining the procedure for an Initial Environmental Evaluation, indicates that applicants for a permit must supply information sufficient to enable the Foreign Secretary to assess, *inter alia*, 'whether there may be alternative ways of carrying out the proposed activity which might lessen the environmental impact or possible cumulative impact'. Assuming that the research in question could be equally well (if more expensively) carried out by a ship-launched AUV, there is always the possibility that a permit would be refused for a shore-based mission. However, there is a strong counter-argument. As an examination of the permit application form for ships reveals (*Report*, Appendix III(2)), the environmental and safety threats posed by conventional ships are substantially different from those arising from the operation of AUVs and there is a good argument for saying that the latter may be dealt with in the course of a section 3 application, as described above.

Reviewing the options open to the UK Government, it seems unlikely that a decision will be taken in the foreseeable future to treat AUVs as ships in law. If this judgment be sound, the onus would fall upon the expedition leaders to make a case for the grant of a permit by demonstrating through a thorough EIA that the shore-based AUV is a research tool which poses no significant threat to the environment; and that the permit procedure applicable to shore-based missions, though different from that applied to ship-based missions, requires a no less rigorous assessment of the environmental impact of the proposed activities.

See further:

- On the general position of AUVs launched from shore, Question 45.
- On other aspects of AUV operations in Antarctica, *Report*, Section 5 and Questions 10, 12 and 13.
- On the legal status of AUVs, *Report*, Section 6 and Questions 15-20.
- On Environmental Impact Assessment, *Report*, sections 5.4.2.5 and 5.5.2.2, and *Guide to Environmental Impact Assessment of Activities in Antarctica* (July 1995, Polar Regions Section, South Atlantic and Antarctic Department, Foreign and Commonwealth Office, London

12. What other protocols, national, or international law may affect AUV operations in Antarctica?

AUV operations in Antarctica are governed by rules of international law, principally laid down in the series of related treaties known as the Antarctic Treaty System, and by rules of national law, most of which are the implementation in national law of the provisions of the Antarctic Treaty System.

The international law regime
AUV operations in Antarctica are subject to the rules of international law governing marine scientific research (MSR) and to the more particular rules embodied in the Antarctic Treaty System.

In principle, the MSR regime introduced by Part XIII of UNCLOS applies in Antarctica. Under this regime, the consent of the coastal State is normally required for MSR conducted in its offshore waters, though the 'qualified consent' rules require consent to be granted for MSR in the waters of the continental shelf and EEZ if specified conditions are satisfied. However, this general MSR regime is significantly modified by the Antarctic Treaty System and in particular by the central instrument of that system, the Antarctic Treaty, 1959. This treaty established freedom of scientific investigation as one of the fundamental principles of the Antarctic regime. The freedom is not of course an absolute one and has to be exercised in accordance with the provisions of the following instruments which make up the Antarctic Treaty System: the Antarctic Treaty 1959; the Convention on the Protection of Antarctic Seals, 1972; the Convention for the Conservation of Antarctic Marine Living Resources, 1980; and the Protocol on Environmental Protection to the Antarctic Treaty, 1991.

The national law regime

In practice, the operator of AUVs in Antarctica need not concern himself too much with the international law regime since AUV operations there will be governed by the rules of national law which have been established to implement international law. Thus, anyone in a British expedition and any British vessel entering the British sector would be subject to the rules and procedures established by the Antarctic Act 1994 and the Antarctic Regulations 1995.

The position is rather less clear-cut in relation to UK AUV operations in sectors of Antarctica claimed by other States. However, in practice, diplomatic clearance has not been applied for and, so far as is known, this has not given rise to any problems, even in times of political difficulty between the UK and Latin American claimant States.

For more detailed discussions, see:

- On the regime governing MSR and the deployment of AUVs in Antarctica, *Report*, Section 5.
- On the Antarctic Act 1994 and the Antarctic Regulations 1995, above Answer to Question 10 and *Report*, sections 5.5.1 and 5.5.2.
- On diplomatic clearance for UK AUV operations in sections of Antarctica claimed by other States, *Report,* Section 5.6.3.

13. Are there any special considerations for operations under ice shelves?

Reference is made to ice-shelves in the definition of Antarctica in section 1(1) of the Antarctic Act 1994. The definition includes 'the continent of Antarctica (including all its ice shelves)' and 'all islands south of 60° S latitude (including all their ice-shelves)'. Neither the Act nor the Regulations made under the Act impose any special constraints on operations under ice-shelves. However, as noted in the Answer to Question 10, permits are required for activities in Antarctica and environmental evaluations have to be carried out. It is always possible, therefore, that the need might become evident to impose restrictive permit conditions following submission of Initial or Comprehensive Environmental Evaluations.

14. What special problems might arise from operations within or close to shipping routes, including shipping routes in straits (narrow straits such as Gibraltar and wider straits such as the Strait of Sicily)?

1. Operations within or close to shipping routes in the various maritime zones

Dealing first with waters which do not form part of a strait, shipping routes may exist in:

- *internal waters*, that is, waters lying landward of the baseline of the territorial sea. The coastal State has sovereignty over such waters and AUV operators in foreign internal waters would require the consent of the coastal State which would be free to subject its consent to whatever conditions it pleased, including prohibition of activities in or near any shipping routes.
- *the territorial sea*, extending to a maximum of 12 nm from territorial sea baselines. Assuming that an AUV is a 'ship', it would enjoy a right of innocent passage through the territorial sea. Passage means navigation through the territorial sea and must be continuous and expeditious. Where necessary having regard to safety of navigation, the coastal State may require the use of designated sea lanes and traffic separation schemes and is obliged only to 'take into account' the recommendations of the IMO; in other words they are not bound by them. AUV 'operations' other than mere passage through the territorial sea would require the express consent of the coastal State which would be most unlikely to be given for operations in or near sea lanes.
- *waters above the continental shelf of a State which has not established an EEZ (where an EEZ exists, see below)*. The consent of the foreign coastal State is required for AUV operations in its continental shelf waters. Assuming such consent has been secured, AUV operations may still be affected by the existence of shipping routes. The fundamental principle governing continental shelf waters is the freedom of the high seas, including freedom of navigation. However, such freedom may be limited where routeing systems have been established under various international conventions, including UNCLOS, the International Convention for the Prevention of Pollution from Ships (MARPOL 73/78) and the Safety of Life at Sea Convention (SOLAS). Details of ships routeing measures are published by IMO. Where such shipping routes have been established, the deployment and use of AUVs would be subject to Article 261 of UNCLOS, under which 'The deployment and use of any type of scientific research installations or equipment shall not constitute an obstacle to established international shipping routes'. AUV operations in or near such routes should therefore be avoided.
- *the EEZ*. Assuming that the consent of the foreign coastal State has been secured for AUV operations in its EEZ, such operations may still be affected by the existence of shipping routes in the EEZ. In essence, the position is the same as that described above in relation to the continental shelf. Freedom of navigation applies in principle but is subject to the constraints resulting from established international shipping routes. Here too, therefore, AUV operations in or near such routes should be avoided.
- *the high seas*. Mandatory, internationally established shipping routes are much less likely to be needed in areas of the high seas lying seaward of the outer limit of

the continental shelf. Where they are established, however, AUV operations should not take place in or near them.
- *archipelagic waters* (that is, the frequently very extensive waters enclosed by straight baselines drawn round archipelagic States like Indonesia or the Philippines). Under Article 53 of UNCLOS an archipelagic State may, with IMO agreement, designate sea lanes for foreign ships passing through its archipelagic waters and adjacent territorial sea. AUV operations should not take place in or near such sealanes.

2. Operations within or close to shipping routes in straits.

If the dimensions and characteristics of the strait are such that there exists through the strait a high seas route or an EEZ route 'of similar convenience with respect to navigational and hydrographical characteristics' to alternative routes through the territorial sea portions of the strait, then ordinary rules governing the territorial sea, the EEZ and the high seas, as explained above, would apply to AUV operations in or near shipping routes established in these various zones of the strait. Assuming that the State or States bordering the straight claim 12 nm territorial seas, the above situation would normally exist where the breadth of the State exceeds 24 nm.

If the strait consists entirely of internal waters and territorial sea (or, in a wider strait, the EEZ or high seas route fails the above similar convenience test), the regime of 'transit passage' will apply in the territorial sea part of the strait if the strait is used for international navigation between one part of the high seas or an EEZ and another part of the high seas or an EEZ. The transit passage regime allows the coastal State, in agreement with IMO, to designate sea lanes and traffic separation schemes, where necessary to promote the safe passage of ships through such straits. Clearly, AUV operations should not take place in or near such sealanes. The right of transit passage (including submerged passage) would be enjoyed by an AUV if it is a ship in law but only for the purpose of continuous and expeditious transit of the strait.

3. Application of specific conventions on routeing and traffic separation

There are specific environmental and safety conventions setting out obligations concerning where ships should navigate, in order that they do not collide with other ships or the shore. The application of these specific conventions partly turns on whether AUVs are ships (see Questions 15 and 16). It seems probable that neither SOLAS nor the COLREGs apply to AUVs so that formally there might not be a need to comply with any specific requirements. Common sense suggests that AUV operators should try to comply with traffic separation schemes or other zoning requirements when AUVs are operating on the surface. In local waters it is far more likely that States will adopt a wide definition of 'ship' so as to apply navigation or traffic management schemes to all sorts of maritime craft, including AUVs.

4. Possible liabilities when operating in shipping routes

Even if, technically, navigational routeing requirements do not apply to AUVs, there is every reason to seek substantial compliance with them, if only to minimise civil liabilities. If an AUV collides with a ship in a busy shipping lane in circumstances where the AUV would be acting contrary to an international or local rule (had it been a ship), there is every possibility that there would be liability in negligence for failing to meet the generally accepted international standards.

For more detailed discussion, see further:

- On *Jurisdiction over MSR in maritime zones, Report,* Sections 1 and 3.2.2.
- On traffic separation schemes, see COLREG 1972, *Report:* Section 7.3.4 and Question 15.
- On international legal requirements for routeing, under SOLAS Chapter V, *Report:* Section 7.3.1 and Question 15.
- On U.K. routeing requirements, see Merchant Shipping (Mandatory Ships' Routeing) Regulations 1997, Question 16.
- On *Ships' Routeing,* the following IMO publications: *Ships' Routeing* (6th ed., 1991, IMO-927E; CD Rom version, 1997, CD-501); *1992 Amendments to Ships' Routeing (1993 edition)* (IMO-924E); *1996 Amendments to Ships' Routeing (1997 edition)* (IMO-921E).
- On legal liabilities of mission programmers, see Questions 33-34

Part D Legal Definition of AUV

15. Under what circumstances and for which laws might an AUV be classed as a ship?

It is important to see whether AUVs are categorised as ships in both international maritime law (see Question 1) and national law (see Question 2).

International maritime law. The question of possible direct application of 'ship' rules to AUVs in 23 specific maritime law Conventions is summarised in Table 2, below: for detailed analysis of how far these Conventions apply to AUVs, see *Report* Section 7.3.

Column 1 of Table 2 lists the relevant Convention (or part of a Convention).

Column 2 indicates in outline how far any definition of a ship in the particular Convention could apply to AUVs and whether there are any other limiting factors (e.g. a tonnage threshold). The general conclusion in the *Report* Section 7.3.24 is that that there is no uniform definition of 'ship' that can be used to decide whether to apply those conventions to AUVs or not. Each convention has its own rules and purposes and it may not always be clear how these will be translated into national law. Similar words of definition may therefore be treated differently in each Convention. The assumptions are based on the present generation of AUVs, such as Autosub. When or if larger and more versatile AUVs are designed, close attention will be needed to see if they fall within the various Convention parameters.

Column 3 in Table 2 is designed to show whether a particular Convention exempts MSR from its coverage, i.e. so that the Convention would not apply even to MSR conducted by a ship. Column 3 assumes use for *pure* non-commercial State activity, e.g. MSR: see further *Report* Sections 3.4, 7.2.

Column 4 provides a brief description of the subject matter of the Convention to indicate how it might be relevant to AUV operation: see also Question 16.

- For the application of specific U.K. laws on ships, see Question 16.
- For the implications of an AUV being categorised as a ship, see Question 17.
- For the position of the deploying ship, see Questions 25 and 45.

TABLE 2

Convention	Application to AUVs	Exception for non-commercial use (MSR)	Relevance to AUV operation (if covered)
SOLAS 1974/1978/1988			• Generally deals with safe construction and operation of ships
Chapter I General Provisions (including definitions)	Probably not 'ship', but see each Chapter Even if 'cargo ship', 500gt threshold	Not generally excepted, but see individual Chapters	
Chapter II Construction	Probably not 'ship' Even if 'cargo ship', 500gt threshold, except for carriage of dangerous goods [Voluntary application of Part 6 of Technical Annex III of ODAS]		• Construction rules, e.g. bulkheads
Chapter III Life Saving Appliances	Probably not 'ship' Even if 'cargo ship', 500gt threshold (300gt for VHF)		• E.g. provision of life rafts
Chapter IV Radiocommunications	Probably not 'ship' Even if 'cargo ship', 300gt threshold		• Types of communication equipment to be installed. • Ability to transmit or receive distress signals • AUVs could not maintain continuous radio watch or comply with manning requirements
Chapter V Safety of Navigation;	Probably not 'ship' No general tonnage threshold	Exception for routeing	• Requirements as to reporting and routing (including VTS); fitting of compass • Use of 'automatic pilot'. If applied to AUVs would require immediate re-establishment of human control, e.g. in high traffic density or poor visibility. In practice AUVs unlikely to be able to comply when on surface

Convention	Application to AUVs	Exception for non-commercial use (MSR)	Relevance to AUV operation (if covered)
SOLAS 1974/1978/1988 *Chapter VI* Carriage of Cargoes	Probably not 'ship' Even if 'cargo ship', 500gt threshold Unclear if carries 'cargo'		• Requirements as to stowage and securing of hazardous bulk cargoes and cargo information provided by shipper,
Chapter VII Carriage of Dangerous Goods (IMDG Code)	Probably not 'ship' Even if 'cargo ship', 500gt threshold [Voluntary application of Part 6 of Technical Annex III of ODAS]		• Requirements as to packaged dangerous goods • Obligations concerning packaging, marking, labelling, stowage and reporting of substances in IMDG Code • May require labelling of AUV modules • Technical Annex III of draft ODAS Convention 1993 recommends exterior labelling of AUV itself
Chapter VIII Nuclear Ships	Probably not 'ship'	Exception	• Assume irrelevant for present AUV operations
Chapter IX Management of the Safe Operation of Ships ISM Code	Probably not 'ship' Even if 'cargo ship', 500gt threshold		• ISM standards relevant to identification of management responsibility for safety • ISM Code relevant to mother ship
Chapter X Safety Measures for High Speed Craft	Probably not 'ship'		• Assume irrelevant for present AUV operations
Chapter XI Special Measures to Enhance Maritime Safety	Probably not 'ship' Even if 'cargo ship', 300gt threshold (500gt for port state control)		• E.g. IMO identification number
Chapter XII Additional Safety Measures For Bulk Carriers	Probably not 'ship'		• Irrelevant

Convention	Application to AUVs	Exception for non-commercial use (MSR)	Relevance to AUV operation (if covered)
Load Lines Convention 1966	Probably not 'ship' 24m threshold		• Rules about buoyancy, stability and freeboard
Tonnage Measurement Convention 1969	Probably not 'ship' 24m threshold		• Used for setting gross tonnage, e.g. for calculating port dues or applying thresholds in other Conventions • May be difficult to apply calculations to AUVs
COLREG 1972	Unclear if 'vessel' Probably not vessel Even if vessel, only when on surface [Voluntary application of Technical Annex II of ODAS, 1984]		• Sets out Collision Regulations for surface navigation • Watchkeeping and lighting rules • Traffic separation schemes • Collision Avoidance systems would need to reflect precise give way rules • AUVs could not comply with watchkeeping rules • Revised Technical Annex II of draft ODAS Convention, guidelines on lights

Convention	Application to AUVs	Exception for non-commercial use (MSR)	Relevance to AUV operation (if covered)
MARPOL 1973/78	Wide definition of 'ship' Means 'vessel of any type whatsoever including submersibles' Unclear if means manned submersible' and may not be 'vessel' But strong possibility that AUVs are within definition Need to look at each Annex	Exception	• Generally to prevent pollution, e.g. through operational restrictions • Reporting obligations if incident with harmful substances
Annex I oil pollution	Even if 'ship', 150/400gt thresholds Not constructed primarily to carry oil in bulk State power to exempt	Exception	• Equipment and operation of bulk oil tankers • Irrelevant for present AUV operations
Annex II noxious liquid substances carried in bulk.	Even if 'ship' Not constructed primarily to carry noxious liquid in bulk	Exception	• Equipment and operation of bulk noxious liquid tankers • Irrelevant for present AUV operation
Annex III pollution by harmful packaged substances	Even if 'ship' Unclear if harmful packages 'carried', or Excluded as 'stores and equipment'	Exception	• Requirements for pollution prevention from hazardous packaged substances • Obligations in packing, marking and labelling, documentation and stowage • Possibly relevant to AUV payloads
Annex IV sewage	Even if 'ship' Irrelevant for present AUV operations	Exception	• Irrelevant
Annex V garbage	Even if 'ship' Applies to garbage, i.e. 'operational waste'	Exception	• Assume irrelevant for present AUV operations
Annex VI air pollution	Even if 'ship'	Exception	• Assume irrelevant for present AUV operations

Convention	Application to AUVs	Exception for non-commercial use (MSR)	Relevance to AUV operation (if covered)
London Dumping Convention 1972/1996	Possibly 'waterborne craft of any type whatsoever'		• Prohibits deliberate dumping • Assume AUVs not disposing of wastes or other matters • Placement (e.g. of modules) for recollection is probably not dumping
OSPAR Convention 1992	Possibly 'waterborne craft of any type whatsoever'		• Framework Convention for pollution in North East Atlantic, e.g. preventing dumping • Requires best available practice and technology • Assume irrelevant for present AUV operations as no dumping carried out
STCW Convention 1978/1995	Probably not 'ship'	Exception	• Regulates training, qualification standards and watchkeeping conduct of seafarers • Seafarer standards requirements irrelevant • Probably forbids autonomous operation of unmanned 'ship' • AUVs cannot meet watchkeeping requirements
Paris MOU 1982	Probably not 'merchant ship' Also depends on application of specific Conventions, e.g. SOLAS		• Binds States to inspect ships entering ports to check international standards

Convention	Application to AUVs	Exception for non-commercial use (MSR)	Relevance to AUV operation (if covered)
Suppression of Unlawful Acts Convention 1988	Possibly 'vessel of any type whatsoever, including submersible' Probably applies only to manned vessels		• Offences for piracy and terrorism. • May provide some protection to AUVs
Intervention Convention 1969/1973	Possibly 'any sea-going vessel of any type whatsoever' Maybe excepted as 'device engaged in exploration of the seabed and ocean floor'		• State powers to give orders and intervene if pollution incident • Rarely relevant as little pollution threat from AUV
CLC 1992 and Fund Convention 1992	Not 'sea-going vessel and seaborne craft, of any type whatsoever constructed for carriage of oil in bulk'	Exception	• Provides compensation for oil pollution damage • Irrelevant
HNS Convention 1996	Possibly 'sea-going vessel and seaborne craft, of any type whatsoever' Probably not carrying listed hazardous and noxious substances as cargo Not in force yet	Exception	• Provides compensation for pollution damage from non-oil pollutants • Might be relevant to insurance cover needed
Draft IMO Bunker Liability Convention	Possibly 'sea-going vessel and seaborne craft, of any type whatsoever'		• Provides compensation for pollution damage from bunker oil • Probably irrelevant as does not carry fuel or lube oil
Draft Wreck Removal Convention 1999	Wide definition of 'ship' Means 'vessel of any type whatsoever including submersibles' Probably covered		• State rights to remove hazards from wrecks • Unlikely to present 'serious hazard' to navigation or environment
Compulsory Insurance Guidelines	Possibly not 'sea-going ship' Guidelines only for national law		• Guidelines as to when insurance against liabilities is compulsory • May be relevant to national law requirements, if any

Convention	Application to AUVs	Exception for non-commercial use (MSR)	Relevance to AUV operation (if covered)
Collision Convention 1910	Probably not 'sea-going vessel'	Exception	• General rules about collision damages claims • Probably relevant to time bars only (e.g. 2 years for claim)
Salvage Convention 1989	May not be 'vessel', but covered as 'property'	Exception	• AUVs can probably be salved, so may have to pay salvage rewards for recovery of AUV • Possible separate liability to pay salvage for owner of payload • AUV can be used to salve other property and claim reward for itself
LLMC 1976	Probably not 'sea-going ship'		• Gives rights to put a cap on any marine liabilities for damages
Ship Registration Convention 1986	Probably not 'sea-going vessel used in international seaborne trade'		• Establishes conditions for registration
Maritime Liens and Mortgages Conventions 1926/1967/1993	Probably not 'vessel'	Exception	• Sets out system of priorities for claimants, e.g. in case of insolvency
Arrest Conventions 1952/1999	Probably not 'sea-going ship'	Exception	• Places restrictions on when ship can be arrested to provide security for civil damages claim
Hague Rules 1924, Hague-Visby Rules 1968, Hamburg Rules 1978	Probably not 'ship' carrying cargo Might be cargo when carried in another ship Exemptions possible Contractual terms may be drafted to include/exclude		• Sets out rights and obligations under contract of carriage of goods.

16. Is there any particular U.K. maritime legislation that could apply to AUVs?

The question of whether general U.K. maritime regulatory law will directly apply to AUVs depends on whether AUVs are classified as "ships" within the Merchant Shipping Act 1995 s. 313(1). It is not possible to be definite without a court ruling, but it appears that English (and probably Scottish) laws and regulations which apply to 'ships' will *not* generally be directly applied to the present generation of AUVs like Autosub (which are incapable of carrying humans). See further *Report* Section 6.4.

There is some indication that the U.K. may take a narrower view of the definition of a ship than other States. In theory, all States should apply the same interpretation to the definitions in the international Conventions listed in Question 15, but in practice they may apply narrower or wider definitions in their national laws with the effect that specific regulations may treat AUVs as ships. The possibility of 'ship' laws applying to AUVs will grow as AUVs themselves increase in size. For the position of the deploying ship, see Questions 25 and 45.

It is therefore perfectly possible that specific Regulations may, by accident or design, have been extended to AUVs. There are hundreds of possible maritime Regulations which could be examined in the U.K. alone and it cannot be said with complete confidence that there are none which apply to AUVs. A selection of recent relevant U.K. maritime legislation is given in Table 3 below to show their possible application to AUVs. This is *not* a definitive list and note that general health and safety at work legislation can apply to AUVs as to any other equipment.

The Merchant Shipping Act 1995 often establishes a framework for details later to be set out in Regulations or Orders. Recent Regulations (1997-) are available free over the web (see http://www.hmso.gov.uk/stat.htm). Increasingly, the Department of Environment Transport and the Regions (DETR) is using Merchant Shipping Notices to set out technical details, e.g. of updates to the IMDG Code, or marine equipment specifications. There are now hundreds of these Notices, some of which are drafted almost like Regulations. Many of these Notices are also available over the web (see http://www.mcagency.org.uk). Note also that the EC is considerably increasing its maritime legislation in the shipping area.

Column 1 of Table 3 lists the relevant U.K. legislation. Column 2 indicates in outline how far any definition of a ship in the particular legislation could apply to AUVs and whether there are any other limiting factors (e.g. a tonnage threshold). Column 3 in Table 3 is designed to show whether particular legislation would have any special relevance to AUV operation, if it did apply to AUVs.

TABLE 3

U.K. legislation	Application to AUV	Relevance
Merchant Shipping Act 1995 s. 313(1)	Probably not a ship	- General definition which applies throughout U.K. merchant shipping legislation, unless context requires otherwise - If AUVs not covered then none of specific sections or Regulations will apply - Note that legislation can apply to operation of deploying ship
Merchant Shipping Act 1995 ss. 85, 86	Probably not a ship	- Safety Regulations issued under ss. 85, 86 would not apply
Merchant Shipping Act 1995 s. 88	Probably only applies to manned submersibles	- Sets out powers to regulate submersibles, including equipment, operation and registration
Merchant Shipping (Registration of Submersible Craft) Regulations 1976	Probably only apply to manned submersibles	- Details of registration requirements for submersibles
Merchant Shipping (Submersible Craft, Construction and Survey) Regulations 1981	Probably only apply to manned submersibles	- Details of construction requirements for submersibles
Merchant Shipping (Submersible Craft Operations) Regulations 1987	Probably only apply to manned submersibles	- Details of operational requirements for submersibles
Merchant Shipping (Cargo Ship Construction) Regulations 1997	Probably not a ship Even if 'cargo ship', 500gt threshold Power to grant exemptions	- Implement SOLAS construction requirements for cargo ships
Merchant Shipping (Carriage of Cargoes) Regulations 1999	Probably not a ship	- Implements SOLAS operational requirements for hazards from cargoes
Merchant Shipping (Dangerous Goods and Marine Pollutants) Regulations 1997	Probably not a ship Power to grant exemptions	- Implement SOLAS operational requirements for pollutants and IMDG Code - Detailed rules on notification, labeling, stowage - Potentially relevant in so far as AUVs carry dangerous goods or marine pollutants in packaged form, i.e. as part of payload.

U.K. legislation	Application to AUV	Relevance
Merchant Shipping (Reporting Requirements for Ships Carrying Dangerous or Polluting Goods) Regulations 1995	"ship" includes vessel of any type whatsoever operating in the marine environment and includes submersible craft Could well apply to AUVs as no apparent restriction to manned submersibles Unclear if AUV payloads are 'goods', as stores and equipment for use on board a ship are excluded Exemption for government of non-commercial purposes Power to grant other exemptions	• Implement Council Directive No. 93/75/EEC, SOLAS and MARPOL requirements on notification to member States of ships bound for or leaving community ports and carrying dangerous or polluting goods (including packaged goods) • Could be relevant to AUV payloads, if treated as goods • Probably most payloads will be excluded as equipment
Merchant Shipping (Mandatory Ships' Routeing) Regulations 1997	Probably not a ship	• Implement SOLAS routeing requirements • Obligation to comply with mandatory ships' routeing systems adopted by IMO
Merchant Shipping (Mandatory Ship Reporting) Regulations 1996	Probably not a ship	• Implement SOLAS reporting requirements • Unlikely to be relevant to AUVs
Merchant Shipping (Navigational Warnings) Regulations 1996	Probably not a ship	• Implement SOLAS requirements on the giving of warnings of hazards, e.g. ice • Obligation on master
The Merchant Shipping (Distress Messages) Regulations 1998	Probably not a ship	• Implement SOLAS distress requirements • Duty of master to respond to distress alert • Unlikely that AUVs could ever assist, and do not have master
Merchant Shipping (Master's Discretion) Regulations 1997	Probably not a ship Probably no 'master' within MSA 1995 s.313(2), i.e. person having command or charge of a ship	• Implement SOLAS requirements • Owner, charterer or manager of ship or any other person cannot restrict master taking decisions necessary for safe navigation • Possibly relevant where management decisions restrict those in charge of AUVs, but difficult to say there is a master
Merchant Shipping (Distress Signals and Prevention of Collisions) Regulations 1996	Probably not ship or vessel Power to grant exemptions	• Implement COLREG 1972 • AUVs could not comply with watchkeeping obligations
Merchant Shipping (Radio Installations) Regulations 1998	Probably not a ship Even if 'cargo ship', 300gt threshold	• Implement SOLAS communication equipment requirements, including automated emergency communications

U.K. legislation	Application to AUV	Relevance
Merchant Shipping (Fire Protection: Small Ships) Regulations 1998	Probably not a ship	• Implement SOLAS fire safety requirements
Merchant Shipping (International Safety Management (ISM) Code) Regulations 1998	Probably not a ship Even if 'cargo ship', 500gt threshold	• Implement SOLAS ISM Code requirements
Merchant Shipping (Survey and Certification) Regulations 1995	Probably not a ship Even if 'cargo ship', 300 gt and 500gt thresholds	• Implement SOLAS requirements on periodic surveys of ships • Requires ships to be detained if do not have appropriate SOLAS certificates
Merchant Shipping (Safe Manning, Hours of Work and Watchkeeping) Regulations 1997	Probably not a ship Specific exemptions may be granted	• Implement STCW Convention • Responsibilities for certification and training of crew and setting of working hours • Obligations in respect of watchkeeping arrangements • Most provisions irrelevant to AUVs, but watchkeeping arrangements to comply with STCW Code. So compliance would be practically impossible
Merchant Shipping (Load Line) Regulations 1998	Probably not a ship AUVs probably covered by specific MSR exemption	• Implement Load Lines Convention 1966
Merchant Shipping (Tonnage) Regulation	Probably not a ship	• Implement 1969 Tonnage Convention • Measurement rules, with volume calculations for ships under 24 m
Merchant Shipping (Registration of Ships) Regulations 1993	Rules exist for small ships under 24m in length and 'submersible vessels' Probably not a ship Reference to 'submersible vessels' is probably to manned submersibles	• Set out requirements for ship registration in U.K. • Probably not possible to register • See Question 18
Merchant Shipping (Light Dues) Regulations 1997	Probably not a ship	• Imposes taxes on ships
Merchant Shipping (Prevention of Oil Pollution) Regulations 1996	"ship" defined to mean vessel of any type whatsoever operating in the marine environment and includes submersible craft Exemption for Government non-commercial service (e.g. MSR) Also Government power to issue exemptions for special craft Some provisions might be theoretically applicable to AUVs 400 gt threshold for surveys	• Implement MARPOL Annex I, e.g. on construction and surveying and maintenance of record books • Most of provisions designed for carriage of oil in bulk so not directly relevant

U.K. legislation	Application to AUV	Relevance
Merchant Shipping (Prevention of Pollution by Garbage) Regulations 1998	Applies to operational wastes generated during the normal operation of the ship and liable to be disposed of continuously or periodically "ship" means a vessel of any type whatsoever operating in the marine environment including submersible craft Could well apply to AUVs as no apparent restriction to manned submersibles	• Implement Annex V of MARPOL • Imposes restrictions on disposal of operational wastes, e.g. in special areas, near offshore installations or in Antarctica • Unclear how far AUV operations generate or discharge operational wastes
Merchant Shipping (Accident Reporting and Investigation) Regulations 1999	Probably not a ship	• Impose duty to report accidents and serious injuries and set out powers of investigators
Merchant Shipping (Port State Control) Regulations 1995	Probably not a ship Exemption for government non-commercial ships	• Implement EC Council Directive 95/21/EC on port State control • Obligations on States to inspect certain numbers of ships and to detain if non-compliance with international standards
Merchant Shipping (Marine Equipment) Regulations 1999	Probably not a ship under U.K. Regulations Under Art. 2(j) of 96/98/EC Directive, 'ship' shall mean a ship falling within the scope of international conventions Probably not a ship within Directive either	• Implement EC Council Directive 96/98/EC of 20 December 1996 on Marine Equipment and 98/85/EC of 11 November 1998 • Require marine equipment to comply with applicable international standards, and establish EC conformity-assessment procedure • Type approval procedures are set out in Merchant Shipping Notice 1734 (M+F), "Type Approval of Marine Equipment (EC Notified Bodies)" and Lloyd's Register is amongst bodies which can approve • Uses an anchor mark to show approval of type • Concerns safety items, such as life-saving appliances, pollution and fire prevention equipment, navigation and communication equipment
Merchant Shipping (Minimum Standards of Safety Communications) Regulations 1997	Probably not a ship Probably not a seagoing ship within Directive and exception for Government non-commercial service	• Implement EC Council Directive 94/58/EC on minimum level of communication training for seafarers

U.K. legislation	Application to AUV	Relevance
Dangerous Substances in Harbour Areas Regulations 1987	Definition means every description of vessel, however propelled or moved. Probably still not a vessel. Not all provisions require connection with ships, so some parts will apply	- Controls carriage, loading and storage of dangerous substances in harbours and harbour areas - Some general parts may be relevant to shore side operations, e.g. on handling of dangerous goods, or notification to harbour master of bringing dangerous goods to harbour - Example of legislation not part of the Merchant Shipping Act 1995, but produced by Health and Safety Executive
Docks Regulations 1988	Not all provisions require connection with ships, so some parts may apply	- Another example of general Health and Safety legislation - Impose health, safety and welfare requirements with respect to dock operations - Might be relevant to shoreside operations with AUVs, but Institute operating Research Vessels will already be aware of general health and safety obligations
Reporting of Injuries, Diseases and Dangerous Occurrences Regulations 1995	No specific requirement of connection with ships, so can apply generally	- Another non-maritime example of general Health and Safety legislation - Obligations to report accidents
Petroleum Act 1987 s. 22,	'Vessels' include 'submersible apparatus', but probably only manned apparatus	- Allows for establishment of 500m safety zones around offshore installations - Offences to enter zones - Does not appear to apply at present, but would be highly relevant if mission accidentally or deliberately takes AUV into zone.
Pilotage Act 1987 s. 7	Probably not a ship. Exemption for ships under 20m	- Provides for compulsory pilotage
Peterhead Harbours Revision Order 1998	AUV covered as a 'thing constructed for…being submersed in water'	- Example of local port legislation. - Allows temporary closure of port areas

17. What are the implications of an AUV being categorised as a 'ship' or not?

If an AUV is a ship it would be subject to national and international shipping law and to those rules of the law of the sea which govern rights of passage through the various maritime zones. See also the Answers to Question 7 (on the rules on innocent passage) and Question 8 (on AUVs navigating between zones).

More particularly, the effect of classifying an AUV as a ship (or vessel), is that a whole range of Conventions and rules which are designed to apply to ships will then be applied directly to AUVs. The precise consequence of applying those individual laws will depend on what each law is designed to do.

Column 4 of Table 2 (Question 15) shows the general relevance of some particular Conventions to AUVs and the sort of implications which will arise for AUV operation if they are treated as ships. Thus, the strict application of the Collision Regulations and the STCW Convention to AUVs would effectively prevent their autonomous surface operation as they would be unable to comply with the watchkeeping requirements. Column 3 of Table 3 (Question 16) also shows the possible relevance of specific U.K. legislation.

Where regulatory rules are concerned (e.g. those laying down construction or operational standards), their application to AUVs will inevitably mean that burdens will be imposed on owners and operators. Instead of being able to set their own standards, retaining scientific or commercial flexibility, they will have to conform to rules set out by someone else. Often, the drafters of those rules (designed for ships) will not have had in mind the particular problems of AUVs.

The consequence of not treating AUVs as ships for regulatory purposes is that many detailed construction and operational requirements (e.g. those for manned submersibles) do not apply to AUVs at present. But it is necessary to look at each Convention and each national regulation to see if some more specific rule has been made applying to AUVs. See further *Report* Sections 7.1, 7.3.24. Thus, even though not ships, AUVs are subject to the law of salvage (*Report* Sections 10.2.3, 7.3.18).

In practical terms, AUVs may operate in a sort of regulatory vacuum.

In general, AUV operators may prefer that they are not subject to detailed statutory regulation, because otherwise they will be involved in costly and time-consuming compliance procedures. The burden is therefore on the AUV community to devise and maintain satisfactory standards themselves, e.g. through the *AUV Code of Conduct* and in applying best available practices.

The absence of formal regulation does not mean, however, that there is no legal responsibility for AUV operation (ignoring moral responsibilities for the moment). There are at least two circumstances where the law will look towards the maintenance of satisfactory standards. The first arises out of the criminal law. Although there may be few formal Regulations setting down construction or operational standards for AUVs at sea, a failure to take care which results in death or injury might result in a criminal prosecution under the general criminal law, e.g. for manslaughter. Secondly, where damage, injury or loss is caused to third parties, e.g. through collision, there may be liabilities under the general civil law. If a court finds that reasonable care has not been exercised, judged by the standards of ordinary competent mariners, scientist and engineers, then considerable damages may be payable (*Report* Section 10). In both of these circumstances, the law will take into account how far AUV operators have identified and operated best available practices. So there is some legal significance in the establishment and maintenance of the *AUV Code of Practice* and compliance with voluntary guidelines, such as those in the ODAS Technical Annexes. Likewise, AUV operators would be well advised to take into account principles set out in the ISM Code.

Most commercial laws apply generally, so they do not depend on AUVs being ships. Thus, the general law of contract (*Report* Section 11) can apply to AUVs and their negligent operation will give rise to liability to third parties (*Report* Section 10.2.1). Exceptions would be rules relating to limitation of liability (*Report* Section 12.2).

- For the position of the deploying ship, see Questions 25 and 45.

18. Is there a requirement in national or international law for an AUV to be registered?

If an AUV is not a ship there is no requirement in current international law for it to be registered, though the establishment of a national Ocean Data Acquisition System (ODAS) register is envisaged in Article 10 of the draft ODAS Convention.

If an AUV is a ship, it would be subject to the rules of international law on nationality of ships. The basic provision is Article 91 of UNCLOS which leaves it to each State, within limits, to fix the conditions for the grant of its nationality to ships and for the registration of ships in its territory. It does not *require* registration of ships and, although registration is the norm for most ships, many States exempt certain classes of ships from the obligation to register.

National law will vary as to whether it is compulsory for ships to be registered and whether there are exemptions for small ships.

For administrative, e.g. customs, purposes, certain States may require that an AUV has some form of identification or Serial Number. In one incident, authorities accepted a Drawing Office Reference Number. So for practical purposes, it may be advantageous to assign a unique number to the AUV.

Under the U.K. Merchant Shipping Act 1995 s. 9, registration is an entitlement not an obligation. On the basis that AUVs are not ships, they cannot be registered in the ordinary way under Merchant Shipping (Registration of Ships) 1993. It also appears that the Merchant Shipping (Registration of Submersible Craft) Regulations 1976 only allow for registration of manned submersibles.

For more detailed discussion, see:

- On the UN Ship Registration Convention 1986, *Report*: Section 7.3.20 and Question 15.
- On the draft ODAS Convention, *Report*: Section 3.3 and Question 3 above.
- On the U.K. Registration Regulations, *Report:* Section 6.6.2 and Question 16.

19. What are the implications of registration or non-registration of an AUV?

Registration of ships performs a number of functions. The main one is to indicate a link between the ship and a State, so that the State of registration (the flag State) can be seen to provide *protection* for its nationals and to exercise *control* over their ships. Protection may be relevant to disputes with other States, e.g. about rights of access. In practice, flag State control implies that burdens will be placed on registered ships, e.g. to conform to safety and environmental standards. These standards should be broadly the same all round the world as they will be based on international conventions, but the detailed rules may vary (see further, Tables 2 and 3 in Questions 15 and 16). More importantly, there is a considerable difference in the way that the laws are *enforced* by certain States.

It might be thought that if registration is voluntary (as in the U.K.), then an owner could avoid regulatory control by leaving the ship unregistered. However, under s. 307 of the Merchant Shipping Act 1995 there is power to extend regulatory control to unregistered ships and the general power to issue safety regulations is also extended to unregistered ships by s. 85(2).

Nationality and jurisdiction.

From the international law point of view, registration of an AUV as a ship (assuming this to be possible) would have the advantage of clearly establishing the nationality and jurisdictional status of the AUV.

As regards nationality, the State of registration would provide documentation attesting that the AUV was entitled to its nationality. This could be very important. It has to be remembered that rights in international law, such as the right to freedom of navigation and the right to freedom of scientific research, belong to 'international persons' such as States and international institutions and not to objects of international law such as ships, companies or human beings. Objects such as ships may enjoy the benefits of such international law rights but only if there is a genuine link of nationality between them and a State. Registration is the normal means of granting nationality. The owner of an AUV registered as a ship could then be comfortable in the knowledge that it would be entitled to the protection of the State of registration if another State were to attempt to deny it the benefits of rules of international law.

Non-registration does not necessarily imply lack of nationality – where for example registration is voluntary under the national law concerned or the 'ship' belongs to a class which is exempt from registration by virtue of its length or tonnage. Nonetheless, on the international plane, registration provides clear evidence of nationality. In the absence of registration, in order to establish that the AUV is of a particular nationality, it would be necessary for the owner to demonstrate a 'genuine link' between the AUV and the State concerned. Normally, it may be supposed that the nationality and geographical base of the owner would constitute the main elements of the link, though complications could arise in the case of inter-State collaboration.

Registration would also mean that, except where otherwise provided by treaty, the AUV would be subject to the exclusive jurisdiction of the State of registration on the high seas.

If and when an ODAS registry is established either nationally or internationally, it might be expected to offer the same benefits as those outlined above.

Commercial implications. There are commercial reasons why owners want to register their ships and these are related to ownership, financing and security.

At a most basic level, the register will provide evidence of ownership and will also impose various formalities about how ownership may be transferred (e.g. according to Schedule 1 of the Merchant Shipping Act 1995). As the register is normally public, its existence may be of some assistance to those who want to trace the owners, e.g. to make a legal claim. If confidentiality of ownership is important (e.g. for commercial reasons), then registration could be a disadvantage. Conversely, registration might assist a Research Institute which wishes to perform MSR in coastal waters as it would demonstrate to the coastal state that the AUV is not owned by commercial interests. In either case, registration will only indicate formal ownership. In the shipping world, it is customary for ships to be registered as owned by a 'shell' company, with the real or effective owner being hidden behind the shareholding in that company, e.g. through holding companies.

In some States, there may be taxation advantages in owning a ship, as opposed to other equipment, e.g. in relation to the basis of computing profits (e.g. by the use of a tonnage tax) or in amortisation period. These advantages might well be linked to registration, but this may not necessarily be so. Banks lending money for the purchase or construction of ships may want to take the opportunity of creating a registered mortgage which is recorded on the register and is given a priority over other claims against the ship (including unregistered mortgages). If an AUV is unregistered, there is no possibility of obtaining this special priority. At present, it does not appear that the financing and construction of AUVs depends on the ability to create a registered mortgage, i.e. that there is a problem in raising finance owing to the difficulty of obtaining a mortgage. See further *Report*: Section 9.1-9.2.

It appears, therefore, as if the factor of registration is of marginal relevance to the commercial operation of AUVs. If an AUV owner did successfully persuade a national administration to register the AUV as a ship, that might then attract many of the international conventions designed for ships (see Question 15).

20. Is there a requirement in national or international law for an AUV to be classified, e.g. with Lloyd's Register, or is it advantageous to do so?

Classification Societies, such as Lloyd's Register, American Bureau of Shipping (ABS) or Bureau Veritas, are private bodies which originally set standards before States became involved internationally in regulating safety of life and in protecting the environment. Classification Society rules typically deal with structural strength and watertight integrity of a ship's hull, and the safety and reliability of the propulsion and steering gear, as well as auxiliary systems on board.

The entry of a ship with a Classification Society, such as Lloyd's Register of Shipping, was traditionally undertaken for the benefit of private interests, i.e. purchasers, mortgagees, insurers and cargo owners who wanted some assurance about the fitness of the ship. The provision of a 100A1 classification at Lloyd's Register, or the equivalent for other classification societies, provided some independent assurance of standards. This assurance may still be an important commercial function where AUV owners need to demonstrate that their craft is constructed and maintained to a particular standard, e.g. where it is hired out, or used to carry a scientific payload. It may be that there are other ways in which insurers and commercial users can become satisfied about the AUV, e.g. by inspection or reputation in a very limited 'market'.

As ships were originally classified for private purposes, there was only a *commercial* obligation to have them classified, e.g. in order to obtain insurance. It may still be important when obtaining insurance to make clear to an insurer that an AUV has not been classed by a Classification Society. Care should be taken to ensure that there is no deliberate or accidental reference in the insurance policy to classification. The standard hull policy for ships (the Institute Time Clauses (Hulls)) makes classification and its maintenance an obligation. So a simple incorporation of these terms (on the basis that AUVs are pretty much like ships) would be inappropriate, without amendment (see further Question 43).

There was no general international obligation to classify ships, as the international construction standards were gradually set down in conventions such as SOLAS, backed up with periodic surveys. In practice, these international standards were also reflected in the rules of the Classification Societies themselves. In some circumstances the functions of Classification Societies appear confusing, as States may have sub-contracted Classification Societies to perform SOLAS surveys on their behalf. Thus Lloyd's Register is an 'appropriate Certifying Authority' under the U.K. Merchant Shipping (Survey and Certification) Regulations 1995. A Classification Society may therefore be performing compulsory surveys under national or international law, but wearing an 'official', as opposed to a 'private' hat.

As a means of ensuring uniformity, SOLAS was amended from 1998 so that in addition to the detailed SOLAS requirements, 'ships shall be designed, constructed and maintained in compliance with the structural, mechanical and electrical requirements of a classification society'. Where SOLAS applies, constructors of 'ships' need to take account of the rules of such Societies. As already indicated (see Questions 1, 2, 15), it does not appear that SOLAS does apply to AUVs as they are not ships. It follows that, unless there are special provisions in any national law, there is no obligation in maritime law for AUVs to be classified.

Although there may be no legal obligation to seek the classification of an AUV, it may still be of some legal importance for AUVs to be designed according to any applicable internal rules of the major societies. One reason is that if there is a liability as a result of any defect, the fault of the designers, owners and operators will be measured by reference to prevailing standards in the industry. AUVs do not fit in easily to the normal Rules of the societies. By way of simple example, the ABS Rules for Building and Classing Steel Vessels 2000, contain a long list of vessel types, none of which directly apply to AUVs (although they might possibly be classified as offshore support vessels). Most societies, such as Lloyd's Register, operate 'offshore registers'. These are designed to cover the variety of special craft used in the offshore oil and gas exploration industry, including small submersibles, with some modifications. AUV interests will need to monitor such rules for their application to AUVs (even by way of analogy) and liaise with the Societies accordingly.

See further,

- On SOLAS requirements, *Report:* Section 7.3.1 and Question 15.
- On liabilities of designers and operators of AUVs, Question 32 and Questions 21-35 generally.

Part E Legal Responsibilities

21. Do the master or owners of the vessel deploying an AUV have any general legal responsibilities?

Although it has been stated that most specific maritime Conventions and national legislation do not apply to AUVs because they are not ships, this does not mean that the general principles of maritime law are irrelevant to AUV activities. This is because a normal ship, often a specialist research vessel, may be used to deploy the AUV. This 'deploying vessel' may be hired in or the AUV operator, e.g. a Research Institute, may use one of its own research vessels.

It is quite clear that the full range of maritime safety and environmental law will continue to apply to the master and owners of the deploying vessel. So they will have to comply with international Conventions and national law. In particular, there will be duties to ensure the safety of the deploying vessel, and personnel on board, including any AUV scientists. So, for an AUV operator which is using its own deploying vessel it will be necessary to take an overall view of safety and environmental regulation. The sanction for failing to fulfil these regulatory responsibilities is that a criminal offence would be committed.

- For liabilities, see Question 25.
- For hiring in of deploying vessel, see Question 27
- For application of international Conventions to AUVs, see Question 15
- For application of national law to AUVs, see (see Question 16)

22. What sort of legal liabilities arise from the operation of AUVs?

We have to be careful about what is meant by 'liability'. It is necessary first to distinguish between criminal and civil liability.

Persons who are subject to regulatory laws, e.g. about safety or the environment, will have a criminal 'liability' (see Question 22). That is, if they fail to comply with the regulatory standards, they may face prosecution and punishment. Depending on national law, there may be punishment of individuals or 'legal persons' such as companies, Research Institutes or Universities. Whether there is a prospect of criminal liability for failing to comply with regulatory standards will mainly depend on the application of specific laws (e.g. on construction or navigation) to AUVs, e.g. are they 'ships'. See further Questions 15, 16 and *Report*: Section 7.

Questions about 'liability' are usually references to civil liability, i.e. the obligation to pay damages by way of compensation for loss suffered by somebody. This liability could arise first, through breach of contract (e.g. between the AUV owner and the owner of a deploying vessel). See further *Report*: Section 11. Secondly, they might arise as a result of liability in the law of 'torts'. 'Tortious' liability (or 'delictual liability' in some legal systems) is just the general description of the categories of liability that can arise between persons who are not in contract. The most common form of civil liability in most legal systems arises as a result of negligence, i.e. fault. Liability in the 'Tort of Negligence' will generally be relevant where there are personal injury claims, or claims for damage to property. It is apparent that AUV operational capacity is presently limited in four areas: navigational accuracy, communications bandwidth, robust mission control functionality and energy storage capacity. All of these limitations could give rise to potential claims in negligence. See further *Report*: Section 10.3.3.

Liability can arise otherwise than under the 'Tort of Negligence', e.g. where specific legislation has created liability of somebody even without the proof of fault. This is known as 'strict liability' and is becoming very common where there are liabilities imposed for environmental damage. See further *Report*: Section 10.2. and Question 30. There may also be liability for breaches of intellectual property rights, e.g. copyright.

Some legal systems, e.g. those on the continent such as Spain, allow criminal and civil liability questions to be decided by the same court, but in the U.K. punishment and compensation issues are generally dealt with separately.

There is no liability simply because there has been negligence. The negligence must actually cause or contribute to loss. See further *Report*: Section 10.2.2.

The range of potential damage caused by an AUV is large, although the risk of it happening might be quite small. The point is that if an AUV did cause damage, e.g. by colliding with a ship, or fouling a seabed pipeline, the extent of any compensation claims could be very high. See further *Report*: Section 10.3. This is the reason why insurance is so important. See further *Report*: Section 13.

There are limits on the extent of any damages recoverable. Thus an AUV owner would not normally be liable for remote economic losses, e.g. where third parties relied on information produced by the AUV. See further *Report*: Section 10.2.1.

23. What is the legal position of individuals working with AUVs (as opposed to that of their employers)?

So far as criminal liability is concerned, individuals, such as masters, may have specific duties placed upon them by legislation. On the basis that AUVs are not 'ships' there is little in the way of specific legislation that would seem to apply to members of an AUV team, apart from the general criminal law, e.g. where death is caused by gross negligence. U.K. law on corporate crime is currently being revised in the light of disasters such as those involving rail transport, so that more criminal responsibilities will be imposed on managers for actions which result in injury or death.

The question arises of how far individual members of an AUV team might face a civil action for damages. There are no particular new liabilities or risks for AUV work, by contrast to ordinary employment. The general position is that an individual who commits the Tort of Negligence is theoretically liable for the consequences, in the same way that there would be liability for negligent driving. The risk to the individual is mitigated by two factors. First, under the principal of 'vicarious liability' an employer is liable for the negligence of an employee committed in the course of employment. In practice, this means that any claimant will sue the employer as it has more resources. Secondly, most employers will carry some form of liability insurance to protect them and their employees if they are sued. See *further* Report: Section 13.

AUV operation may pose risks of injury or damage to third parties. Even if these risks are more uncertain in scope than those which arise with traditional MSR, the individuals should feel assured that any legal problems will generally be for the employer and its insurers.

- For liabilities to third parties, see *Report:* Section 10.3.
- For vicarious liability, see *Report:* Section 10.2.4.

24. Is there any difference between the legal position of an AUV owner, an AUV operator, an AUV hirer and an AUV manufacturer?

Lots of organisations will have a connection with an AUV, but their position in civil law will vary, depending on whether one looks at their relationship between themselves (usually determined by contract), or their position in relation to others (sometimes described as 'third parties') with whom they have no contract.

As between themselves, they will have rights to make use of the AUV, most of which will be regulated by contract. The manufacturer will generally have rights in the AUV until paid. Thereafter, the owner will obviously have the primary right to control what happens to the AUV, although it may give temporary rights of control to a hirer. In some cases, the AUV may be legally owned by one entity, although operational decisions in respect of it are taken by another related, but legally separate, organisation. E.g., a Government Research Institute may own the AUV, but it may be operated by a University Department. All the rights and obligations owed by the various parties can be adjusted between themselves by appropriate contractual clauses, e.g. hold harmless clauses.

As against third parties, any of the persons connected with an AUV can have liability in 'tort', usually for the negligence of an employee. In general, their legal position will depend on the extent of any control that they have over activities concerning the AUV. That is, they will be liable because individuals they employ have been at fault.

- AUV Owner: The presumption will usually be that the Owner will generally be liable to third parties for negligent actions or decisions concerning AUV operation taken by its employees. It will not be liable for the negligence of the master or crew of a deploying ship, unless they are also employees. So the AUV owner would normally be responsible for the decisions about missions taken ashore, or on board any deploying vessel. See further *Report*: Section 10.2.
- AUV Operator: Any individual 'operator' actually controlling the AUV in real time will be liable for negligence, as will their employer. But there might be an organisation or unit which manages the operation of the AUV for another

organisation, but which is legally separate from it. This rather nebulous category of 'Operator' could also have liabilities. Particular risks of liability occur when negligent mission planning or programming is undertaken. Although not an owner of the AUV, this Operator could be liable if there has been a negligent input into the operation of the AUV. See further *Report*: Section 10.3.4.

- AUV Hirer: A hirer of an AUV will probably not generally be liable for any faults committed by the AUV Owner, e.g. in construction or maintenance. The extent of the hirer's liability will depend on the degree of its own control over operations and its own negligence. A hirer which takes the bare hull of the AUV will be liable itself if it negligently programmes a mission. Where there is joint fault with the employees of the Owner, then there could be joint liability. See further *Report*: Section 10.2.4.
- AUV Manufacturer or designer: Any manufacturer or designer could be liable in negligence, or under product liability laws if faulty design or manufacture has actually caused loss. See further Question 30 and *Report*: Section 10.2.2. If this fault is compounded by the negligence of the owner or operator, then there could be joint liability.

In all the cases described above, the various persons may be directly liable to third parties, but may then (afterwards) adjust those liabilities between themselves by contract.

- For contractual indemnities and hold harmless clauses, see *Report*: Section 11.4.5 and Question 41.
- For liability for negligence of an employee, see *Report*: Section 10 and Question 24.

25. What are the liabilities of the Owners and Master of a vessel deploying an AUV?

Neither the *Report* nor these Questions and Answers focus on the duties and liabilities of the owner of the deploying vessel, as such. Rather the concentration is on the owner or operator of the AUV. In order to give detailed legal advice, about such duties and liabilities, to the owner of a deploying vessel it would be necessary to consider the whole of maritime law designed for ships. That would not be possible, so only a brief answer can be given.

Criminal liability. The *Report* and these Questions and Answers have concentrated on the AUV as it acts autonomously, but close attention would have to be paid as to whether the AUV can be treated as part of the equipment of the deploying vessel. In some circumstances, it is conceivable that the owner and master of the deploying vessel would be covered by maritime safety legislation in circumstances where the AUV owner would not. Owners and masters who fail to comply with regulatory laws applying to their own deploying vessel, e.g. about safety, will have a criminal 'liability'. Thus, rules about safe stowage aboard the deploying vessel could apply to the latter when the AUV was being lashed on the deck of the vessel. Similarly, when in the act of deploying, the deploying vessel would have to comply with the Collision Regulations. That vessel would probably be classified as a 'vessel restricted in her ability to manoeuvre' within Rule 3(g) while deploying. The vessel would have to display particular lights and shapes and use special sound signals. Rule 18 gives certain privileges to this sort of vessel, except (for instance) in narrow channels or traffic separation schemes.

Civil liability. The master (or crew members) of the deploying vessel could theoretically be sued for their own negligence, but this is unlikely.

The civil liability of the owner of the deploying vessel could arise in contract or tort. Liability could arise through breach of contract (e.g. with the AUV owner). An example might be where the Owner and crew of the deploying vessel failed to take care of the AUV so that it was damaged. The vessel itself might suffer an engine failure so that time was lost. In both these cases, the legal rights and obligations, and the consequences of breach, ought to have been allocated between the parties through a contract.

Liability could arise in a number of ways in the Tort of Negligence to pay damages by way of compensation for loss suffered. The vessel may be navigated negligently while attending or deploying the AUV, so that there was a collision with another ship. This would be the legal responsibility of the owner and master of the deploying vessel. As a result of the negligence of the crew of the deploying vessel, there may be death and personal injury to the vessel's own crew, or to a member of the scientific team accompanying the AUV. Again, this would be the legal responsibility of the owner and master of the deploying vessel. In some cases, there might possibly be joint fault of the AUV team and the crew of the deploying vessel, e.g. in the provision of information about the properties of the AUV which resulted in injury while it was being loaded or deployed. Both sets of employers would be liable to any third parties.

It is possible to imagine circumstances where that master of the deploying vessel is negligent in allowing the AUV team to deploy the AUV, or to let it be operated in particular areas. The master may be aware there are other vessels in close proximity, or know that AUV operation might cause special problems to other persons or property in the area. Essentially, the fault of the master here would be one in relation to safe navigation. The master will always have the final say about the safety of his ship and he may be held at fault if he allows his ship to be used as a platform for activities which threaten the safe navigation of others, e.g. where an AUV team insist on deploying the AUV, or programming it to run, when the master thinks it unwise.

- For criminal liability, see Questions 21, 22.
- For civil liability of individuals, see Question 23.
- For liability to any third parties, *see Report*: Section 10.3.
- For allocating liabilities by contract, see *Report*: Section 11 and Question 41.

26. What is the legal liability position where the owner of the AUV and the owner of the deploying vessel are the same?

The point here is that, as the owner is the same, it will normally be the employer of all those connected with both the AUV and the deploying vessel. It will have to take account of the ordinary maritime rules applying to ships and their equipment (see Question 25). As an employer of personnel, it will be liable for the negligence of all of them, although the liability cannot exceed the damage or loss which has been caused.

However, care will still need to be taken when dealing with insurers, as there will probably be different insurance policies covering the deploying vessel and the AUV itself.

From a tactical point of view, it may be preferable legally for any fault to be laid upon the deploying vessel, as this will certainly be entitled to limit its liability to third parties according to a statutory formula based on the size of the ship. If, however, there is also fault in relation to the AUV (e.g. in negligent programming or real time operation) then it seems that there will be no possibility of limiting liability in respect of the AUV, as it is not a 'ship'. If an AUV team is negligent, it might be possible to treat them as effectively as members of the crew of the deploying vessel, so that their actions arise in direct connection with the operation of the deploying vessel. In this case the employer could limit liability. The limits are only likely to be relevant in the case of a very high claims, e.g. where there is damage to a subsea pipeline.

- For limiting liability of deploying vessel, see *Report*: Section 12.2.
- For limiting liability for AUVs, see *Report*: Section 12.2.2.
- For limitation of liability amounts, see *Report*: Section 12.2.5.

27. What is the legal liability position where the owner of the AUV hires in a deploying vessel?

There are three common types of charterparty (i.e. contract) for the use of a ship: demise (or bareboat) charters, time charters and voyage charters. These resemble, respectively, a car hired from Avis by the day, a chauffeur driven limousine hired by the day, and a taxi hired for a particular journey.

Each of these charters involves different contractual obligations for the parties between themselves. Care needs to be taken in drafting to ensure that exclusions or limitations of contractual liability are acceptable and that hold harmless indemnities can be covered by insurance.

In terms of liability to third parties (including death and personal injury to employees and crew members), there is a significant difference between demise charters and the other two. A demise charter involves the hirer in taking a bare hull (hence bareboat charter) and operating it entirely with its own personnel. The hirer would then be liable for any negligent operation of the vessel. It seems unlikely that a Research Institute would be able (or wish) to demise charter a specialist research vessel without a crew, although it might possibly demise charter a smaller support ship to operate as a deploying vessel for an AUV. The point is that the hirer would have full liabilities for the operation of the ship and would need appropriate insurance. A Research Institute would not become a demise charterer simply because it has employees on board the deploying vessel, e.g. where a scientific team accompanies the AUV. In these circumstances the owner of the deploying vessel would be responsible for the faults of its employees and the employer of the AUV team would be responsible for their negligence. That employer would probably be the AUV owner, but that is not necessarily so (see Question 24): vicarious liability attaches to the employer of persons negligent, rather than the AUV as such.

If a deploying vessel is time or voyage chartered, it comes along with the master and crew. The owner of the deploying vessel, and not the AUV owner, will be responsible for their negligence. Of course, the AUV owner can be liable if there is also negligence referable to the employees of the AUV owner (e.g. where an AUV team negligently programmes a mission, whether aboard a deploying vessel or ashore).

A breakdown may occur in equipment on the deploying vessel which is used to communicate with the AUV. This may result in some third party damage, e.g. where a mission cannot be aborted. In those circumstances, it would seem that the owner of the deploying vessel will be liable to the third party. The AUV owner would probably not be liable, if it had no control over the equipment, it maintenance or use. It is possible that a court might hold that there was a degree of joint enterprise, so that the AUV owner was also liable. It is for such reasons that it is important that the contract for the use of the deploying vessel allocates liabilities between the parties, after they have settled the third party claim.

- For hold harmless indemnities, see *Report*: Sections 11.2, 11.4, 11.5 and Question 41.
- For demise charters, see *Report*: Section 11.2.1.

28. What is the legal liability position where the owner of the AUV uses a deploying vessel belonging to a collaborating partner where no formal contract or agreement may exist?

Two Research Institutes may collaborate in a mission, perhaps as a result of a joint funding bid to a research council. It is theoretically possible that the arrangement between the two Institutes does not involve a contract, even though nothing may be signed. See further Question 38. In most cases the courts will probably imply basic contractual obligations, e.g. that each party will take reasonable care. If an employee of the AUV owner was injured through the negligence of the crew of the deploying vessel, the injured employee would have to sue the owner of the deploying vessel. In terms of the ordinary employer's cover for injury while at work, it might make sense for each employer to assume the ultimate responsibility for satisfying the claims of its own employees. This could be achieved by contractual indemnities. So, if only for insurance reasons, it is advisable for some written contract to be prepared.

As against third parties, the position will be broadly the same as that where a deploying vessel is hired in under a time or voyage charterparty. Each of the Institutes will be liable for the faults of its own employees. It seems likely that there would be a much closer degree of co-operation between the Institutes than there would have been if a deploying vessel had been commercially engaged. This raises the possibility that there would be a greater scope for any third party to prove that there was joint liability for AUV operations generally. Once again, contractual hold harmless clauses will clarify the position as between the two Institutes as to who ultimately should bear any loss.

- For insurer's rights and contracts, see *Report*: Section 13.1 and Question 38.
- For time and voyage charters, see *Report*: Sections 11.2.2, 11.3.3 and Question 27.
- For hold harmless clauses, see *Report*: Section 11.4.5.

29. Does the legal liability position vary where the owners of the AUV and the owner of the deploying vessel are in based in different States?

The fact that the AUV owner and the owner of the deploying vessel are situated in different States raises the possibility that the law applicable to any disputes is different in those States.

As between the two owners, it is essential that any contract contains an express choice of law and jurisdiction clause. This will ensure that there is no doubt about the law which governs the contract, and the court (or arbitral tribunal) which will hear any dispute. Naturally, most people are happier to stay with the devil they know and each party may want to insist on its own law and jurisdiction. There are significant costs involved in all legal cases, but litigating in a foreign system can be time consuming and expensive. One advantage for a U.K. based operator is that a choice of 'English law and jurisdiction' is customary in many maritime contracts and London is recognised as generally providing a fair venue for international parties. Chauvinism apart, it is strongly advisable to insist on an English law and jurisdiction clause, at an early stage. Insurers would also be unhappy if agreements are made subject to foreign law.

Where liabilities to third parties are involved, there is less scope for agreeing upon the appropriate legal system to govern disputes. If an AUV were to cause property damage or death and personal injury there would obviously be no advance choice of law. Here, there is a strong possibility that any third party claimant would want to sue in its State, according to the law of that State. The point here is that this risk of suit in a foreign court does not arise because of the nationality of the owner of the deploying vessel, as such, but because operations are undertaken overseas which present the risk of damage or injury to foreign nationals. It may well be that a foreign collaboration is being sought because MSR is to be undertaken in areas of the world with which the foreign owner is familiar, or close to where it is based. The fact that the foreign owner is based in a separate State also increases the possibility of a third party claimant taking legal proceedings in that State, because it will be easier to gain access to the assets of that owner. The risk of legal actions in different States is simply one of those facts of life in shipping. Once again, it emphasises the importance of having insurance cover, which will also cover legal costs.

While AUV owners and operators may be focussing on liability for property damage, the greatest exposure may well be through death and personal injury. Although the AUV has no crew, it needs to be loaded, discharged and deployed and could theoretically damage another craft and pose a risk to persons there. It is notorious that damages awarded by US juries in death and personal injury cases are higher than anywhere else in the world. Compensation claims could run into millions. For that reason, care needs to be taken in any contract that could conceivably involve a US connection, or the use of US nationals. Not only will insurers expect to be informed of missions with a US connection, but the contract will have to be drafted to ensure that appropriate indemnities exist.

- For choice of law and jurisdiction clauses, see *Report*: Section 11.4.6 and Question 46.
- For insurance cover, see *Report*: Section 13 and Question 42.
- For contractual indemnities, see *Report*: Section 10.3.2 and Question 41.

30. What are the liabilities of the manufacturer of the AUV?

The liability of the manufacturer of an AUV will be no different in principle from the liability of any manufacturer.

The extent of any liability to the purchaser will be determined by the contract of sale. A manufacturer would generally be obliged to provide a product which met the sale description and was fit for any purpose which had been specified. It would be perfectly normal for the manufacturer to seek to exclude or limit certain liabilities by express terms. In English law these would generally have to pass a test of 'reasonableness'. It would be common to exclude certain consequential loss (e.g. where any defect in the AUV caused delay to a mission and large disruption costs) and/or to limit any liabilities to a certain sum, e.g. the contract price or some other figure. That figure will very often be tied to any insurance cover taken out by the manufacturer, say for £50,000 per incident.

Towards third parties there can be a liability in the Tort of Negligence for defects which cause death and personal injury. In some circumstances there may be liability for foreseeable property damage, although most legal systems will restrict the extent to which the manufacturer would be liable for consequential (economic) loss. If the defective design or manufacture of an AUV caused an operational failure, e.g. where the propulsion system would not cut out and the AUV collided with an offshore oil installation, the manufacturer could be liable to the owner for the costs of repairing the installation, but possibly not for financial losses caused to others who wanted to use it.

Many legal systems now have special legislation on 'product liability'. The EC Product Liability Directive 1985 (85/374/EEC) has been enacted in the UK in the

Consumer Protection Act 1987. It was originally designed to protect consumers from products such as Thalidomide and is primarily designed to give a remedy for death and personal injury. The legislation creates strict liability upon the manufacturers of defective products and would extend to AUVs. It would apply if there was injury caused to someone handling an AUV where the injury resulted from a defect in its construction. There might also be injury from leakages of chemicals from some of the scientific modules. If the component was supplied to the producer of the AUV by a sub-supplier, that person may be liable. A person who merely uses a product, e.g. someone who charters an AUV, will not be a producer and will have a defence. So far as property damage is concerned, the Act only creates strict liability for property damage where the damage exceeds £275 and that property is of a description ordinarily intended for private use or consumption. This would exclude most of the property damage that could conceivably be caused by a defective AUV, except perhaps where damage is caused to a yacht. See further *Report* Section 10.2.2.

A difficult question is to decide what is a 'defect' in a product under the Directive or 1987 Act. The defect will relate to any perceived risks. One of the design risks concerns 'blind' surface navigation and it is arguable that this would be a defect. The Consumer Protection Act 1987 s. 4(1)(e) provides a 'state of the art' defence to the producer. However, it seems that this relates only to defects which the producer might not have been expected to *discover*. In the case of 'blind' navigation, the defect is obvious; it is the remedy that is the problem. It seems that a person injured as a result of 'blind' navigation might have a claim against the manufacturer. The person who buys a product such as an AUV does not then have the strict liability of the manufacturer, and there is also a defence where a person never 'supplies' the product to another. So, if a Research Institute designed and built an AUV itself for its own use it would not have a liability under the Directive or 1987 Act (although it could still be liable in the Tort of Negligence).

A manufacturer would expect to cover product liabilities through specific insurance policies.

- For programming liabilities, see *Report*: Section 10.3.3 and Questions 33-35.
- For insurance generally, see *Report*: Section 13.1 and Question 42.

31. What are the liabilities of a designer of an AUV where manufacture is entrusted or licensed to another?

A designer might incur third party liabilities in a number of ways.

First, the 'client', e.g. a Research Institute, may commission the construction of the AUV from an engineering company. Here there is a difference between supplying specifications to a manufacturer, which then uses those to design the final form of the AUV, and actually providing the manufacturer with a finished design so that the AUV can be produced with little or no further re-engineering. In the former case, it will be the manufacturer which has liabilities to any third parties.

If the design has been negligently produced by the AUV client (e.g. so that there is failure of an AUV's steering system, causing injury), then the latter will be liable in negligence. The manufacturer might also be liable under strict product liability legislation. In either case, it may well be very difficult to say that it was only one party or the other that was responsible for the design, as the manufacturing process may have involved considerable input from manufacturer and AUV client. In these circumstances, the AUV client will be responsible for its own negligence. It may also possibly be liable for failing to detect defects in the designs provided by the manufacturer, provided that these could have been discoverable by the exercise of reasonable care. In all these cases, the contract for design or manufacture should set out the obligations of both parties to each other and how third party liabilities will be settled.

Secondly, a designer could license its own copyrighted design for an AUV (or component or module) to a manufacturer for commercial production. Where third parties are later damaged or injured through a defect in design the manufacturer might again be liable under strict product liability legislation. The contract between the parties should deal with these liabilities and state how far the manufacturer should be indemnified. The designer could also be liable directly to the third parties in negligence for foreseeable loss.

Thirdly, there may be liabilities arising out of the design, not of the structure of the AUV, but of a computer program used in specifying the mission. Here again, there may be liability of the person responsible for the production of that program, which may not necessarily be the AUV owner. The AUV owner will probably only be additionally liable in negligence if it should have discovered the defective program through the exercise of reasonable care.

- For manufacturers' liabilities, see Question 30.
- For programming liabilities, see *Report*: Section 13.3.3.Questions 24, 33.

32. What are the liabilities of the user of the AUV?

There may be many different persons who could be 'users' of an AUV. In essence, the liability to third parties of any person using an AUV will depend on whether that person (or any employees) have been guilty of negligence. See generally Questions 21, 24.

A user may be aware of the risk of loss caused by the inherent design limitations of AUVs (e.g. as to navigational accuracy, communications bandwidth, robust mission control functionality and energy storage capacity). If it decides to operate the AUV knowing of that risk, then however much it tries to limit any damage it will almost certainly be treated as negligence if loss results from that known risk.

- The owner of an AUV will often be a user and will be liable as such in negligence. See generally Question 24, 33.

- A user who has hired out the AUV as a bare hull and has used its own employees to program the mission and handle the AUV will be liable for the negligence of those employees. See *Report* Section 11.3.1.
- A user who has hired out the AUV with a team will continue to be liable for any negligence of its own employees. The AUV team will not normally be treated as the employees of the hirer, unless for some reason the hirer has actually taken them on the payroll. Defects in the AUV itself will be the primary responsibility of the AUV owner. If the AUV team is negligent, e.g. in downloading mission programs, then it is the AUV owner which will be primarily liable. See further *Report* Section 11.3.2.

Users of an AUV can incur liabilities in contract through the use of the AUV. An oil company (X) may need to perform surveying work as part of a larger contract with oil company Y. If it hires in an AUV from Research Institute Z, and (for some reason) the AUV fails to perform the work, oil company X could be liable to Y in contract. For that reason it may want to sue Z under the X-Z contract. It is therefore important that all parties know what are their respective rights and liabilities under the contract, whether the arrangements are truly back to back and whether the liability of Z is in any way excluded or limited.

- For negligence in failing to maintain standards, see *Report*: Section 10.3.3 and Question 14.
- For contractual protection, see *Report*: Section 11 and Question 41.

33. What are the liabilities of the person(s) programming the mission of the AUV?

Apart from inherent defects in the design of any computer program (see Question 31), there can be liabilities if a mission is negligently programmed and this causes loss.

The liability would primarily fall on the employer of the negligent programmer (see Question 23). The negligent programmer may not necessarily be employed by the AUV owner, but could be a employed different Research Institute. See further *Report* Section 10.2.4 and Question 24.

There may be potential breaches of contract (e.g. where the AUV is hired with a team to perform a survey for a client) and a program does not achieve the promised result. See further *Report* Section 11 and Question 41.

Alternatively, negligent programming could cause the AUV to take a wrong course so that it collides with an object (e.g. a ship, or a fixed installation such as a pipeline, or jetty) belonging to a third party, thereby giving rise to liability in the Tort of Negligence. See further *Report* Section 12 and Questions 14, 22. Negligent programming here would include simple errors in inputting data, so that a 'wrong', i.e. unintended, course was taken. Negligence would also occur when the programming achieved exactly what the programmer intended, but where those objects were judged not to take reasonable care for the safety of others. The programmer will need to have a wide knowledge. See further Question 34.

Liability could also arise as a result of the inherent limitations of AUV design. For example, if an AUV is navigating on the surface and is unable to detect, or react to, the presence of other craft it might be considered negligent to allow it to operate without any anti-avoidance program. This may not be the fault of the programmer, as such, more that of the AUV owner in permitting the AUV to operate 'blindly'. In other circumstances the programmer might be at fault in the programming of any abort missions. The simplest programme may well instruct the AUV to remain floating to enable it to be recovered, or to take a pre-determined surface course. If the AUV mission is then aborted and it is hit by a passing ship, that ship would claim that it was negligent to allow the AUV to remain a surface hazard to other craft. The AUV owner might try to argue that there was no negligence, as the reason for aborting the mission had occurred without fault (e.g. failure of GPS links) and that the abort program was the most reasonable solution for a variety of unforeseeable circumstances. Although such a defence is arguable, it may be unlikely to find favour with the courts. See further *Report* Section 10.3.3 and Questions 25, 24, 32.

34. Is there any special knowledge that the mission programmer should have in order to minimise legal liabilities?

The mission programmer must obviously be aware of the area in which the AUV is programmed to operate or where, as a result of an abort order, it might operate. See further *Report* Section 10.3.3 and Question 33.

Although the navigation and watchkeeping rules of the Collision Regulations, SOLAS and the STCW Convention might not strictly apply to the navigation of AUVs, that does not mean that these standards are irrelevant for liability purposes. The contrary is true. The standard of care required in negligence actions is that of the reasonably prudent person in a similar position - here the reasonably prudent operator of an AUV. The courts would measure the standard of care to be expected of AUV owners and operators by reference to the standards applicable to shipowners, making due allowance for any differences resulting from the nature of AUVs.

The main problem would seem to be surface navigation where there is a risk of collision with other craft. The mission programmers should therefore be fully aware of the appropriate rules for navigation of craft on the surface and should know about when craft should 'give way' to other craft.

- For the application of SOLAS and the STCW Convention, see Questions 15, 16.
- For standards of care generally, see *Report* Section 10.2.1. and Question 35.

35. How might these programming liabilities be affected if the AUV alters its own mission plan, e.g. due to a collision avoidance manoeuvre or due to feature tracking?

It follows from the Answers to Questions 34 and 35 that it may be no answer to a claim caused by AUV contact that 'as the vehicles are autonomous, we obviously cannot see where they are at all times and cannot control them in all circumstances. We did our best'. The courts would not allow AUV operators to pass onto other users of the oceans the risks of allowing AUVs to run blindly. In the unlikely event of an AUV colliding with another craft while navigating on the surface, or while surfacing to communicate, the courts would almost certainly hold that it was negligent to take the risk of a collision if the AUV had no reliable means (at least equivalent to a human lookout) of detecting and reacting to the presence of other craft. If the AUV was fitted with an automatic collision avoidance system (properly programmed), this would be some evidence of the exercise of reasonable care so as to assist a defence to a negligence action. In contrast, the absence of any such system, or something equivalent, is likely to be viewed of itself as lack of care.

The question implies that, despite any collision avoidance system, the AUV may collide with another craft or fixed or floating object. Each case would have to be determined on its own facts, but the obvious questions would be why did the collision then occur? It may have been because the other craft could not react to the navigation of the AUV because it could not be detected, e.g. at night. Assuming that there was no negligent lookout on the part of the other craft or object, the fact remains that the AUV owner has still put into the water an object which is difficult to detect and which may not have any function at least equivalent to a human lookout.

It may be a defence to a negligence claim to prove that there was such severe weather that even a manned ship would have been out of control, but these circumstances may be rare. It is no defence, as such, to point to a mechanical failure and then to say that thereafter the programming could have done nothing to prevent a collision, as the courts will focus on why the failure occurred in the first place. Even where the mission was aborted, it might be no defence to say that the mission programme did all that could be expected, i.e. to signal the position of the AUV so that it could be recovered. To that extent, the AUV owner may not be able to hide behind a 'state of the art' defence, any more than could the operator of an autonomous road vehicle which could not avoid other cars.

- For standards of care generally, see *Report* Section 10.2.1. and Questions 30, 32, 33, 35.

36. How might false claims for salvage be avoided?

Under the 1989 Salvage Convention there seems little doubt that an AUV will be treated either as 'vessel' or 'any other property in danger' at sea. See further *Report* Sections 7.3.18, 10.2.3.

The 1989 Convention does not apply to 'non-commercial vessels owned or operated by a State' and it might be possible to claim sovereign immunity. However, there are doubts about the application of this immunity to AUVs (are they 'vessels'?) and not all AUV activity is non-commercial. See further *Report* Sections 3.4, 7.2, 7.3.18. It seems unlikely that the U.K. would claim immunity for AUVs as salvage is allowed of HM ships.

On the assumption that an AUV is 'property' capable of salvage, it must be in 'danger' for a salvor to claim a reward. In law, danger is a question of fact and a mistaken belief that there was danger will not be sufficient, although danger does not have to be immediate and it would be enough for a salvor to show a reasonable apprehension of loss or damage in the absence of help. There may be a number of circumstances where the AUV is apparently immobilised, so that it appears to a discoverer to be in danger, although it is in fact still operating according to programme. Thus, although an AUV on the surface in daylight awaiting a navigation fix might appear 'dead' to a potential salvor, it would not be in danger (unless perhaps in the middle of a busy shipping lane). The same conclusion would probably apply if an AUV is temporarily immobilised and waiting to be retrieved after an aborted mission. Here it would be necessary to enquire whether there was a reasonable chance that the AUV might drift aground, as immobilisation in circumstances where there are likely to be physical risks to the AUV will be considered as danger. There have been examples of persons 'finding' lost naval sonars or buoys and claiming that they have saved them from danger. The AUV may be perfectly safe in the sense that it is programmed or designed to sit on the seabed. A fishing vessel which merely 'captured' an AUV in its nets would not automatically be entitled to salvage, particularly if the AUV was still operating autonomously at the time. In most of these cases, there would have to be difficult negotiations about the nature of the risks involved and whether danger was reasonably apprehended by the salvor.

It is highly advisable, therefore, to follow the Autosub practice of having a statement printed on the casing which says, 'Harmless Scientific Instrument. If found, contact [XYZ]'. Such a notice might serve to dispel any reasonable apprehension of danger arising from the AUV being lost or abandoned, at least where the AUV was merely unattended. The clearer the information on the casing, the better. Of course, if the AUV was being lashed against a rock, it would still be in danger, whatever was written on the casing: similarly, if there had been a power or communications failure which meant that the AUV was effectively 'lost' to its owner.

The AUV owner must decide whether the greater need is to encourage communication from discoverers or to avoid honest (or spurious) salvage claims where there is in fact no danger. To assist the latter objective, it might be advisable to say a little more on the casing notice about danger not *from* the AUV ('harmless') but *to* it. Thus, a statement could be added along the lines of 'This Instrument is pre-programmed [to conduct experiments on the surface and underwater] and is capable of sending and receiving satellite messages. It is not in danger merely because it is immobile on the surface or on the seabed. If in any doubt, please contact....'.

In any negotiations with discoverers, it should be pointed out that the person who finds property such as an AUV in danger, does not become its owner, although there will be an entitlement to a reward based on the value of the AUV. The tactical bargaining position of a salvor is quite strong in that it has a 'maritime lien' for its services and can retain possession of the salved AUV. The AUV owner faced with a salvage claim is probably best advised to contact its insurer immediately. The usual marine policy should cover salvage claims and the insurer will expect to provide security (e.g. a guarantee) to enable the AUV to be released. The insurer may instruct specialist lawyers to advise on what is a reasonable reward. Assessing the reward requires independent advice. AUV owners should be aware that a salvage reward is *not* calculated on some fair rate for the work performed, i.e. a sort of daily rate hire, but is designed to encourage salvage operations by being generous and is based on the *value* of the property salved. Thus, if an AUV valued at £500,000 was salved, that sum would be the *maximum* possible reward. Although that would never be awarded in practice, it does indicate that substantial sums might be payable. In a case where the AUV had been completely lost to its owner without hope of recovery, a substantial reward could be expected, e.g. up to 50%- 70% of the salved value. In cases where the risks were less, a considerably lower sum might be awarded, but AUV owners should be thinking in thousands, not hundreds, of pounds.

Liability for salvage does not depend upon there being any contract at all, or even any communication between the salvor and the owner of the AUV. The right to a reward arises by operation of law on the performing of a service to maritime property in danger. Where there really was a danger, it might be advisable to consider going to arbitration by signing a Lloyd's Standard Form of Salvage Agreement (LOF). However, AUV owners should not sign such a contract in circumstances where they wish to dispute that there was ever any *danger* at all. Before agreeing to an LOF the AUV owner needs to consult the insurers and may have to take specialist advice.

Where an AUV is immobilised, and theoretically in danger, there is an alternative to agreeing a salvage contract. There is nothing to prevent the AUV owner from arranging itself to have a contractor recover the AUV under an ordinary contract. This would be a 'no-salvage' recovery contract, probably agreed for a fixed price and not dependent on a 'no cure: no pay' arrangement. In these circumstances the contractor would not be able to claim salvage as well, nor should its crew have a separate claim. It might be possible to require the contractor to give an indemnity against possible crew claims. For a simple operation it may not be necessary to agree anything too sophisticated, although consideration should be given to the issues mentioned in Questions 41 and 46. There are a number of possible standard form contracts available, mainly designed for large scale wreck raising, including the new 'Wreckstage 99' lump sum stage payment contract, the 'Wreckhire 99' daily rate contract, or the 'Wreckfixed 99' fixed price contract. The latter is a 'no cure: no pay' agreement. Wreckstage 99 is probably the most suitable, but with appropriate amendments. The AUV owner would have to pay the cost directly and it may not be covered by the insurance policy. By contrast, if the AUV owner accepts salvage services, this may be covered by insurance.

It might be tempting to try to offer a small sum to the discoverer of an AUV which was not considered to be in danger, but some care will be needed here. First, the insurers may decline to provide an indemnity for this sum unless they have been contacted. Secondly, the offer needs to be made expressly on the basis that there was no danger and no salvage. Thirdly, if the claim is made, for instance, by the owner of a fishing vessel each crew member may have an individual claim to share in the reward and the fishing vessel owner cannot deprive them of it. This presents practical problems, as if the payment to the fishing vessel owner is not for salvage the crew have no claim to share in that money and may therefore press on with a salvage claim. So some assurance will be needed that any payment to the fishing vessel owner will cover all crew claims. Once again, the advice is to obtain specialist legal advice while consulting the insurer.

- Note that an AUV may itself perform salvage services
- For details of the requirements for a salvage claim, see *Report*, Section 10.2.3.

37. Are there special contracts for using AUVs?

There are no special rules of contract applying to AUVs: the ordinary rules of contract of a particular State will apply (see further, *Report*, Section 11 and Question 2, above).

In practice, it will be very important to settle in advance standard terms that will apply for the use of AUVs. The type of terms and the form of the contract will vary depending on which kind of contract is being made. Thus, there may be:

- Contracts to use somebody else's ship to carry the AUV (including charterparties of ships). See further *Report* Section 11.2.
- Contracts to hire out the AUV alone. See further *Report* Section 11.3.1.
- Contracts to hire out the AUV with a team. See further *Report* Section 11.3.2.
- Contracts to perform a service for a client, e.g. sea-bed surveying. See further *Report* Section 11.3.3.
- Contracts to carry a scientific payload belonging to someone else in the AUV. See further *Report* Section 11.3.4.

For some contracts, such as charterparties of ships, there are internationally accepted standard contracts. The 'Supplytime 89' time charter is a contract that is used for hiring supply vessels in the offshore industry and can be adapted for use in hiring ships on a daily rate to carrying out missions with an AUV. It is probably advisable to have a basic contract for each of the bulleted contracts, above. Many of the clauses will be similar.

38. Do we always need a contract?

Where there is an agreement between two organisations for the use of equipment, such as an AUV, there will, in law, probably be a contract. This is so even where no formal written document is drawn up and a contract can be concluded on the telephone, or by fax. For this reason, it is important to be clear what the terms are and to use, or refer to, standard form contracts.

Even where there are informal collaborative agreements between Research Institutes which do not involve commercial profit, but the use of vessels or equipment, the courts may imply that a contract exists. The reason is that there are so many possible rights and duties that may arise that it would be difficult to regulate them without some sort of implied bargain. The fact that money does not change hands is not decisive, as the arrangement may be more like barter. One Institute may hire a Research Ship from another friendly Institute to carry an AUV and the scientists involved may be old colleagues who prefer to make arrangements as informal as possible. If something goes wrong (e.g. the AUV or ship is damaged, or someone is injured, or there are bad weather delays) there may be liabilities. The Institutes may be content to rely on their insurance policies. The point is that the insurers themselves may want to sue the other party, to recover their payouts, even though the parties do not want legal action. Insurers have the right (subrogation) to sue in the name of the policy holder, but they will be bound by any contract that has been made (as they stand in the shoes of the policy holder). For this reason, it is important to be as clear as possible in contractual arrangements, even informal ones, as these will bind the insurers. Care must be taken, however, to ensure that insurers are informed in advance of all contracts which might take away their rights.

- For methods of agreeing contracts, see Question 40.
- For standard form contracts, see Question 41.
- For informal collaborative arrangements, see Question 28.
- For insurers' rights and contracts, see *Report* Section 13.1.

39. Do we have to employ a lawyer to draft AUV contracts?

Not necessarily! It helps if a lawyer has given general advice about basic clauses to use for normal operations. At the very least there has to be someone who has responsibility for considering the terms of the contract and the appropriate negotiation procedures.

It is all too easy to assume that the agreement is all about settling technical issues, e.g. performance specifications, and that these are the only relevant matters for settling any charges. But all agreements can result in liabilities where something goes wrong. If the operation of an AUV causes an accident resulting in death, personal injury or property damage there may well be costs involved which go beyond the value of the AUV or the contract price, e.g. where third parties make a claim. In these circumstances, the parties need to be clear who is going to bear the risk, as between themselves, and to insure accordingly.

Risk allocation in contract is normally performed by clauses which exclude or limit liability. For example, if a vessel is hired as part of a MSR mission to carry an AUV, it will be common for each party to exclude liability for any loss or damage to the vessel or AUV, as the case may be. Further, if a ship's crew member is injured while handling an AUV, that person might sue the AUV owner. It would again be common to include an indemnity clause whereby the AUV owner (if liable for negligence) would pass on the liability to the vessel owner by relying on the express indemnity clause. This arrangement might be commercially sensible as the vessel would expect to be insured for injury to its crew. Taken together, the exclusions and indemnities are often referred to as a 'hold harmless' agreement.

- For contract negotiations, see Question 40.
- For standard form contracts, see Question 41.

40. When should we raise legal issues about contracts?

AUV operations are not conducted for lawyers and the scientific and financial components of any mission are obviously the main issues. But experience shows that it is necessary to consider the allocation of legal liabilities at an early stage (e.g. with 'hold harmless' clauses). This will be particularly important when the other side (e.g. an oil company) has based negotiations on its standard contract. It may be very difficult in practice to make late changes to such a contract when it has been approved by that company's in-house lawyers. Accepting liabilities by contract can impose significant cost risks and these have to be factored into any agreement.

- For contract negotiations, see *Report*: Section 11.1.2.

41. Which legal issues should we consider when drafting contracts involving AUVs?

The key points are to identify the risks which might be involved in a particular contract and to decide how to allocate them. If a standard form contract designed for another mission is being used, take care to see that the risks are the same.

The following is a *brief* checklist:

- Who are the parties to the contract? See further *Report* Section 11.1.1.
- When do you want the negotiations to become binding? Are arrangements 'subject' to any event, e.g. formal signing of a contract, or approval from superiors? See further *Report* Section 11.1.2.
- If you are in a chain of contracts (e.g. where subcontractors are involved) are you sure that the arrangements are 'back to back'? See further *Report* Section 11.1.2.
- Whose standard terms are being proposed? Are you aware of the differences between your standard form and the one proposed by the other side? See further *Report* Section 11.1.2.
- Is the standard form contract suitable for this particular mission? See further *Report* Section 11.1.2.
- Have you agreed to achieve 'absolute' results, even when prevented through no fault of your own, or only accepted duties to take reasonable steps? See further *Report* Section 11.3.2, 11.4.1?
- How have you allocated 'force majeure' risks, e.g. bad weather? See further *Report* Section 11.2.2, 11.4, 11.4.2.
- Who is liable for delay? See further *Report* Section 11.2.2.
- Who is liable for damage to property and death or personal injury, including that suffered by third parties? See further *Report* Section 11.3.1.
- Which costs will be extra? See further *Report* Section 11.2.2.

- Have you considered rights to terminate the contract and when they will arise? See further *Report* Section 11.4.2.
- Have you considered whether it will be possible to calculate any damages, or whether it might save trouble to specify them in advance? See further *Report* Section 11.4.3.
- Which consequential losses are possible and has liability for them been allocated? See further *Report* Section 11.4.3.
- Does the contract exclude liability of either party, e.g. for any loss or damage to the AUV? See further *Report* Section 11.4.4.
- Are there any indemnity clauses in the contract? See further *Report* Section 11.4.5.
- Are the exclusions and indemnities (i.e. a hold harmless agreement') covered by insurance? See further *Report* Section 11.4.5.
- As an AUV owner, has a vessel operator issued you with a bill of lading or waybill? See further *Report* Section 11.2.4.
- Have you included an express choice of which court shall have jurisdiction, whether to have arbitration and which legal system will be used to resolve disputes? See further *Report* Section 11.4.6.

42. Is it compulsory or merely advisable to insure an AUV?

Most employers will be required to carry normal insurance cover for liability to employees, e.g. under the Employers' Liability (Compulsory Insurance) Act 1969. At present, the only international requirement for compulsory insurance at sea is for oil tankers. There is no equivalent of the compulsory third party cover which exists for road use.

So there is no Convention which currently *requires* an AUV to carry insurance cover, although there may possibly be requirements in national laws. Section 192A of the Merchant Shipping Act 1995 gives the U.K. power to require that a contract of insurance shall be in force while a 'ship' is in U.K. waters. As it appears that AUVs will not be treated as ships, even this power could not be extended to AUVs, unless the U.K. declares AUVs to be ships under s. 311 of the Merchant Shipping Act 1995. Even then, there will be exceptions for ships being used for non-commercial purposes.

Although there is no requirement to carry insurance cover, it is highly recommended that AUVs should be insured. The insurance will cover two broad risks: loss of the AUV itself and liabilities to third parties. The property insurance of the AUV is unlikely to be covered under a general insurance policy, e.g. for equipment. If it is generally included, it will probably not be covered for *marine* risks. It is also extremely unlikely that the AUV will be included under the ordinary hull cover of a Research Ship which is used to transport it, as the AUV will not be treated as equipment of that ship. For this reason a separate policy will almost certainly be needed. Of course the AUV owner may decide to accept the risk of the loss of its craft and many Governments have a policy of not insuring State property.

The really important insurance cover is that which covers potential risks to third parties. These liabilities could arise as a result of negligence.

- For international compulsory insurance cover, see *Report*: Sections 7.3.14 - 7.3.16 and Section 13.1.
- For treatment of AUVs as ships, see Questions 1, 2, 15, 16.
- For U.K. powers to extend definition of ship, see Questions 2, 16.
- For property insurance cover, see *Report*: Section 13.2.
- For liabilities in negligence, see Questions 21-35.

43. How should AUV insurance be arranged and is there any special form of insurance for AUVs?

It is generally advisable to consult an insurance broker, preferably one specialising in marine risks. The broker will then advise on the form of policy which should be agreed, but as noted in Question 42, above, the policy will have to cover both damage or loss to the AUV itself and liabilities to third parties.

For Research Institutes which already operate their own ships, it would be sensible to contact the same brokers or insurers, as there is a possibility of arranging the AUV cover as an addition to the ship's hull and machinery policy. If the owner is entered in a P & I Club the AUV might possibly be covered under the Club rules, but in practice it is more likely that a separate policy will be arranged for the AUV. This will essentially be a hull policy covering marine risks with added liability cover.

There is no special policy designed for AUVs, as such, but the key point is that it is unlikely that insurance cover can be bolted on to an ordinary employer's liability policy. It is likely that, on the London market, insurance would be offered under the Mar (91) form, with detailed clauses added to cover marine risks (e.g. there should be a special mention of salvage). As these clauses may have been reworked from a policy designed for a ship, close attention will be needed to ensure that wording designed for the commercial operation of ships is fully suitable for AUVs on scientific missions (see also Question 20 on classification).

It is important that the insurer is given the fullest possible information about the AUV, its design, construction, management and operation. In particular, the insurer will need to know the geographical areas of operation. Advance agreement on payment for entry into particular areas should be discussed, e.g. in US waters. If the AUV is subcontracted to work need offshore rigs or pipelines, the insurer would expect to have been informed.

Where contracts are being used for the carriage of the AUV, or its utilisation (e.g. for commercial purposes), the insurer should be consulted about the form of any contracts, for instance as to hold harmless arrangements envisaged. If possible, draft exclusion and indemnity clauses should be approved by the insurer and a mechanism discussed for obtaining approval of any clauses which may be offered by other contractors.

Where collaborative arrangements are likely with other Research Institutes, the insurer should be asked about giving waivers of its subrogation rights, or how far it is possible for other persons involved in a mission to be named as 'additional assured' under the policy. Thus, the policy may cover the liabilities of employees of the owner of the AUV (or whichever entity takes out the policy), but scientists from a legally separate Research Institute may be involved in aspects of the mission such as programming. The original policy could name such persons, or a mechanism could be agreed to add them as additional assured so that they would be protected. There have been legal doubts about how far such persons could claim the benefit of the policy, to which they were not parties, but it seems as though the Contracts (Rights of Third Parties) Act 1999 will now assist them. Where an AUV is being carried on board a deploying ship, it may also be worth inquiring whether that ship's insurers are prepared to include the AUV or its team as additional assured. In some cases there may be duplication of cover, but this may not be unacceptable unless extra costs are involved.

- For hold harmless agreements, subrogation and insurers, see *Report*: Sections 11.4.5, 13.1
- For salvage, see *Report*: Section 10.2.3
- For hull and machinery cover, see *Report*: Section 13.2.1
- For liability cover added to hull policy, see *Report*: Section 13.3.1

Part E Legal Responsibilities

44. What identification marks should an AUV carry and what warning signals should be provided when on the surface and when submerged?

The answer to this question will depend, in part, on whether an AUV is treated in national or international law as a 'ship'.

So far as international law is concerned, if an AUV is a 'ship', the required identification marks and warning signals would be those provided for in the relevant international conventions, including:

UNCLOS. Articles 90-93 refer to the national flag and Article 94 to the duties of flag States, including the duty to take measures necessary to ensure safety at sea. These rules do not refer to particular identification marks or warning signals.

The Collision Regulations. The Rules apply to 'vessels', which include every description of water craft used or capable of being used as a means of transportation on water (Rules 1(a) and 3(a)). Part C specifies 'Lights and Shapes'. Rule 23 specifies lights for power-driven vessels underway. Compliance with the principal prescription in this rule, which includes a masthead light, would appear to be impracticable but vessels of less than 7 metres in length and whose maximum speed does not exceed 7 knots may instead exhibit 'an all-round white light' and, 'if practicable', sidelights. Rule 27 prescribes more complex requirements for 'vessels not under command or restricted in their ability to manoeuvre' (defined in Rule 3) but here too vessels of less than 7 metres in length are not required to exhibit the lights prescribed in this Rule.

The better view probably is that an AUV is not in law a ship. If this is so, it must be said that it is very difficult to point to any rules of international law which prescribe precise identification marks or warning signals. However, UNCLOS provides a general rule and further guidance is available in the form of internationally agreed guidelines for the adoption of national measures to ensure the safety of Ocean Data Acquisition Systems (ODAS).

So far as UNCLOS is concerned, Article 262 provides that scientific research installations or equipment deployed or used in the marine environment 'shall bear identification markings indicating the State of registry or the international organisation to which they belong and shall have adequate internationally agreed warning signals to ensure safety at sea…, taking into account rules and standards established by competent international organisations'. Pending the establishment of a register or registers for ODAS or AUVs, there is, strictly speaking, no 'State of registry' but it would be in keeping with the spirit of this passage to require markings identifying the vehicle with a particular home State.

Article 262 indicates that account is to be taken of standards established by competent international organisations and here it is appropriate to refer to a draft Convention on ODAS and to Technical Annexes attached to it, prepared by the Intergovernmental Oceanographic Commission (IOC) and the International Maritime Organisation (IMO). Although the draft Convention is still only a draft, its Article 16 points in what is probably the right direction. It requires that a submarine ODAS which, due to the depth at which it is deployed, 'constitutes a danger to shipping or navigation or to fishing', must either be escorted by a vessel capable of giving due warning to passing ships, or be provided with effective signals as set forth in Annex II.

As has been noted in the Answers to Questions 3 and 7, Annex II is one of three Technical Annexes to the draft Convention on ODAS which were published separately so that, pending the conclusion of a Convention, States could use them on a voluntary basis as guidelines for national measures. As was seen, an updated version of Annex II on *Marking and Signals* was circulated in 1985. Annex II makes provision for both identification marks and lights and signals.

As regards 'identification and marking', this model would require:

- The clear display on an exterior surface where it can best be seen of an alpha numerical identification consisting of a unique identification number prefixed by the letters ODAS (arguably AUV would serve equally well) and suffixed by letters indicating the State in which it is registered (in the absence of a registry, the home State might be indicated). A replica of the flag of the State may also be painted on or applied to the exterior surface as a further optional means of identification.
- If feasible, the name and address of the owner should also be displayed.
- Surface-penetrating AUVs would have 'their visible positions' (in practice their entire surface) painted yellow.

Reference must be made to Paragraph 2 of Technical Annex II for details of 'Lights and Signals' but the main requirements may be summarised as follows:

- The lights and signals have to be positioned in places where they can best be seen or heard.
- A satisfactory radar response at a distance of at least 2 miles must be ensured for AUVs constituting a danger to shipping and safe navigation.
- Surface-penetrating AUVs must exhibit from sunset to sunrise a yellow flashing light visible all round the horizon, with, where technically feasible, a nominal range of at least 5 miles.
- They must also carry a sound signal where its installation is technically feasible.

Even though the above recommendations may not be compulsory, it is advisable to comply with them, if only from the point of view of minimising potential legal liabilities. If an AUV were involved in a collision where its visibility was an issue, the fact that it had complied with the only available international standards would be of some relevance to a negligence claim.

For more detailed discussion, see further:

- On whether an AUV is a ship in law, *Report*, sections 6 and 7.
- On the Collision Regulations, *Report*, Section 7.3.4.
- On the draft Convention on ODAS and Technical Annex II, *Report*, Section 3.3 and, for the text of Technical Annex II as revised in 1984, Appendix IB of *Report*.
- For liabilities, *Report*, Section 10 and Questions 21-35, especially Questions 33-35.

45. If an AUV is launched from shore, how does this affect the issues discussed in this Report?

1. International law of the sea.

So far as the international law of the sea is concerned, the fact that an AUV was launched from shore would underline the fact that this was indeed an *autonomous* vehicle. To put it another way, there would then no longer be any question of considering the AUV as being part of the research equipment of a mother ship or of being cargo of a ship. This would affect the public law issues discussed in the *Report* as follows:

- *In relation to securing consent from foreign States for MSR by the AUV in their waters*

The coastal State has sovereignty over it internal waters, territorial sea and (in the case of Archipelagic States) archipelagic waters and its express consent is required for MSR conducted by foreign AUVs in these zones. Given the novelty and lack of a track record of AUVs, it is to be expected that many States will regard foreign AUVs as posing threats to the safety of shipping and offshore industries; national security; and the marine environment. Such fears might exist even if the AUV is deployed from a mother ship but it would obviously be easier to provide assistance in this case. The fear must be that many States would refuse consent for MSR by unescorted AUVs in their waters.

The position is less clear cut in relation to MSR by AUVs in the EEZ or continental shelf waters of a foreign States. The coastal State does not have an absolute discretion to withhold consent and, indeed, the general rule is that 'in normal circumstances' consent has to be granted for MSR. However, the rules governing this 'qualified consent' regime do not refer specifically to AUVs and, in referring to the 'methods and means' and 'scientific equipment' to be used, seem to assume the presence of a research vessel. Whether foreign States would accept that unescorted, unsupervised AUVs constitute such research vessels may be doubted. It would also be open to them to argue that 'normal circumstances' did not exist if unescorted AUVs were operating in their offshore waters.

- *In relation to rights of passage through the various maritime zones*

As was noted in the Answer to Question 7, an AUV would be entitled to the right of innocent passage through the territorial sea of a foreign State only if properly considered to be a 'ship' and this is doubtful. Similar problems would arise in relation to rights of 'transit passage' through straits and 'archipelagic sealanes passage' through archipelagic waters. Even the freedom of navigation in the high seas and in EEZ and continental shelf waters would be in doubt since these freedoms too are enjoyed by 'ships'.

- *In relation to State practice and procedure, including the need for a climate of trust in relations with foreign States*

State practice indicates that the consent of foreign States to MSR in their waters can be more readily secured if trouble is taken to build up a climate of trust between the foreign State authorities and those of the requesting institution. The burden of creating such a climate would be considerably heavier in cases where the research is to be conducted via unescorted AUVs.

- *In relation to operations in the Southern Ocean and Antarctica*

The problem of AUVs launched from shore in Antarctica is dealt with in the answer to Question 11, above.

2. National law.

In terms of national law, there may be two issues, one regulatory, the other concerned with liability.

If the AUV is launched from within a port, it may be subject to the local port legislation which may impose restrictions on operations, e.g. that launching is subject to the permission of the harbour master. This local legislation can vary from port to port.

Where there is only an AUV involved, and no deploying vessel, it is obvious that it can only be the AUV owner who will generally be liable if the AUV causes any damage or loss. There also seems far more opportunity for such damage or loss to occur in a crowded port. See further *Report*: Section 10.3. The AUV owner will not be able to limit liability by statute. See further *Report*: Section 12.2.

46. How might legal disputes be settled?

1. Disputes under international law

Three scenarios may be envisaged:

(i) Where the AUV is deployed from and closely attended and supervised by a mother research vessel. In this case, *the rules on dispute settlement* referred to below would apply.

(ii) Where the AUV (however launched) is not closely attended and supervised by a mother research vessel and it is operating 'autonomously'; and it is accepted by both sides that it is in law a ship. In this case, the 'nationality' of the AUV could be determined and the AUV would then be subject to the jurisdiction, and entitled to the diplomatic protection, of its home State. If, then, a foreign State acted in breach of the rules of international law in relation to the AUV (by, for example, denying it access to its waters to conduct MSR), the owners/operators of the AUV could refer the matter to the home State for dispute settlement on the international plane in accordance with *the rules on dispute settlement* referred to below.

(iii) Where the AUV (however launched) is not closely attended and supervised by a mother research vessel and it is operating autonomously; and it is not considered to be a ship in law. In this case (and assuming that the AUV has no other link of nationality through, for example, registration on a future ODAS registry) the position is more difficult. Arguably, the owner of the AUV could seek the diplomatic protection of the owner's home State. However, given the uncertain juridical status of the AUV and doubts as to its entitlement to conduct MSR, the prospects of proceeding in this way would not be promising

The rules on dispute settlement. Assuming that scenario(i) or scenario (ii) applies, what are the relevant rules on dispute settlement? In fact, the rules of international law on dispute settlement are very complex and would be a matter for the Government of the home State rather than the owners/operators of the AUV. A new system of dispute settlement was introduced by Part XV of UNCLOS and offers a variety of alternative mechanisms, including the International Court of Justice, the new International Tribunal for the Law of the Sea and arbitration.. The mechanisms available for settlement of any particular dispute would depend upon the scope of declarations on 'choice of procedure' made by the States parties concerned. That is the general position. It has to be noted, however, that the coastal State may take advantage of a very significant escape clause in Article 297(2) of UNCLOS, whereby it may exclude the application of these mechanisms to MSR disputes. Where the coastal State exercises this option, the AUV home State will be left without a binding dispute settlement procedure, though in certain cases it may have resort to a process of 'conciliation', the result of which is not binding.

For more detailed discussion, see further:

- On *Settlement of MSR disputes*, *Report*, Section 3.2.5 and E D Brown, 'Dispute settlement and the law of the sea: the UN Convention regime'. 21 *Marine Policy* (No. 1, 1997), pp. 17-43, esp. at p. 21.

2. Regulatory disputes

There may be a dispute with a national regulatory authority about whether, or how far, specific rules on ship operation should be applied to AUVs. In the U.K. it will be necessary to have discussions with the Maritime and Coastguard Agency. If the authority proposes to apply ship rules in such a way as to cause serious disruption to AUV operation then, after political approaches have failed, it may be necessary to take court action for a declaration as to whether the authority's action is lawful. Such action will be expensive and is therefore to be discouraged. If an authority decides to prosecute an AUV owner then the criminal law courts will be the forum for the dispute.

3. Disputes involving AUV liabilities

Most lawyers would advise against becoming involved in litigation, owing to its cost and delay, and will nearly always recommend that parties compromise (settle) their claims. There are now alternative forms of dispute resolution which the parties are encouraged to use, including mediation.

Where there are contractual relationships, commercial parties may often prefer to opt for arbitration where the parties, in effect, choose their own judge. The decision whether to accept arbitration needs to be made on a case by case basis. In some circumstances arbitration can be quicker and cheaper than going to court, but this may not always be the case. London is a leading centre for maritime arbitration and London arbitration might be acceptable when ships are chartered. For disputes about whether data produced by an AUV meets any contract specification it might make sense to agree that the dispute should be arbitrated by a neutral scientist or engineer, or a panel composed of one arbitrator nominated by each side with an umpire nominated by the arbitrators if they cannot agree. As arbitrators must be paid, the decision about whether to use a panel has cost implications. Although the decision about whether to use arbitration is usually agreed in a contract in advance of any dispute, it is perfectly possible to agree to arbitration after the dispute has arisen.

If it is not possible to resolve disputes amicably then the only alternative will be to go to court. In international disputes it is vital to be able to decide on two issues:

- Whose court will determine any disputes (jurisdiction), and
- Which law (e.g. English or US law) will govern that dispute (governing law).

In contracts it is absolutely essential to provide expressly for a 'choice of law and jurisdiction clause' or a 'choice of law and arbitration clause'.

- See further, *Report*: Section 11.4.6 and Question 29.